MW00644199

Have Bikini
Will Cruise

Splashy Stories of the Seven Seas

Gail Endelman Small

LESS
WORDS
PRESS

Published by Less Words Press, an imprint of WavoMedia
2060 D Avenida de Los Arboles #590
Thousand Oaks, CA 91362
www.LessWordsPress.com

First Edition, 2021

ISBN: 978-1-947028-01-2

Library of Congress Control Number: 2021917678

Cover design by: DJ Geomatics

Printed in the United States of America

Contents

Preface

From the frantic moment of a lost bikini to an incredible encounter with a head of state, there are so many adventures and misadventures to share. So, with travel to seven continents and the seven seas, there is much to be told. Now for a few hints of what will be revealed through the true stories of cruising in this book ...

First a confession! As an experienced world traveler, I got lost in a foreign land. (And on a cruise ship too.) I have strung popcorn in the middle of the night and have been mercilessly strung along by a comedian. I have found joy wandering narrow streets in foreign ports as well as paddling in a canoe to unknown places in the pouring rain. I have shared mishaps and zany encounters with friends old and new. It is all part of the fun and almost indescribable adventure.

You're going to meet some special people in my life. My son, Michael Whiteman, who crewed on a sailboat across the Pacific is now grown, though we share wonders of the world. My mom, Miriam Small, has passed, though her love of travel and resilience is a part of the cruises I take. And, my cartographer and cartoonist husband, David Endelman, who I kidnapped into the world of cruising.

I love the discovery element in my travel adventures and the camaraderie of meeting people on a ship. There is something magical about being on the ocean. The possibilities in cruising are endless. The stories and memories came alive once more even as I wrote them. Maybe they will touch you with your own memories or future cruise dreams. I hope to meet some of you, fellow travelers, on a future cruise. For now, let's enjoy some wanderlust!

The Why

The trees swayed with a gentle mist while the waves swelled in a sea as blue as can be. We grasped the ambiance and allure of Hawaii while celebrating the thrill of cruising. Next stop, Ensenada, and my visit across town to my favorite tortilla lady where I have gone for years. Being my hometown is on the outskirts of Los Angeles, Ensenada has been an easy access getaway since I was a teen. The smell of the warm corn tortillas, like a delicacy, and the sight of them flipping into the air was so satisfying.

Nighttime came with a return to the ship for the last night's gala events and … packing. I was on my way home, always sad when a trip comes to an end, though Chile was weeks away. Time to unwind, though not much, and Dave and I were packing to speak in South America, first stop, Chile. Not!

Just as we were about to catch our international flight, we realized that suddenly cruising was not an option, not even a possibility. Word of a cruise suspension spread, ships stopped, and an unknown virus named Covid-19 was apparent. My tears flowed amidst my frustration of this unforeseen abrupt change and not being able to return to South America.

They say things happen for a reason. Not something I could reason with at the time! We learned that travelers were stuck in Santiago as well as ports across the world. So, our cancellation was meant to be. We were not trapped anywhere except in the disbelief of being safe at home with fully packed suitcases and speeches ready to deliver. Our thoughts went out to those at risk and the many unable to return home because of the closing of international borders.

Since that very day in March 2020, dialogue on disappointment and the yearn for cruising was heard online and amidst friends and acquaintances everywhere. Trips were canceled and the future unknown. Illness hit many and some sadly lost lives. How fortunate many of us truly are when looking at the total situation. Compassion becomes the key. The crew has been far from their homes and loved ones while at sea with not knowing an outcome for days, weeks, and months. The crew brings the delight and enjoyment of cruising with their caring and energy. They needed to be protected, helped ... and appreciated. Repatriation is what was needed the most.

Thus, comes this book of my memoirs. To bring joy and remembrances to cruisers and a positive take on cherished cruising. Many of us can all recall once-in-a-lifetime laughs, leisure, and navigation to infinite possibilities. The moments and mishaps. I stopped counting cruises a while ago after I got to 101. I am happy that cruising can now begin again. Cruising will be different and is resuming as safe, reasonable, and ready with the new modern-day "normal."

There was a pause as ships around the globe were waiting … Going on a cruise or any adventure, one is always full of anticipation. Things don't always go the way you think they will go. Keeping calm with an open attitude sure helps one and all. Have fun and be f-l-e-x-i-b-l-e …

FYI- The sound of the horn is the most exhilarating part of cruising for me. Just to know the ship is about to sail. Whether the first port or the last, there is elation to hear the blasting sound. I can't wait!

Through the true stories I share, please reflect on your dreams of future travels and the cherished memories of voyages and adventures!

How It All Began

How do we all get so busy? It happened to me, teaching in a multi-aged program as well as lecturing at local colleges and more. Somehow days fly by, yes, they do.

My mom always was a fan of Bernadette Peters and I read that she was appearing in San Francisco. Hmm ... a plan! Plane tickets were doable, and the flight is less than an hour from Los Angeles. I reserved tickets to the show and a hotel room.

We spent that weekend loving the show and the moments relaxed for a change, together. Many know of Bernadette Peters because of her signature curly hair. She is though award-winning and so multi-talented; she dazzled the audience in her remarkable show. "Pennies from Heaven" is her song that floats through my mind from time to time. Also, as an animal lover, I applaud Bernadette Peters for her dedication and founding of "Broadway Barks." She is known for her charity work and her rescue dogs.

Mom and I always shared a strong bond. I appreciated her caring and strengths that were multiple. I talked to Mom often and visited her for a family lunch or dinner when our schedules worked. Holidays were shared and celebrated. This was different because of the real quality time for just us, together. That weekend get-away set the stage that there is no better time – to enjoy one-on-one time with someone special.

Thank you, Bernadette Peters! For thirty-three years, once a year, Mom and I reserved a special time together. It didn't matter what or where, we would get creative as the time together was what was important. Sometimes we laughed, sometimes we cried, and we wandered together to many places and shared priceless memories.

The First Time I Ever Walked on a Cruise Ship

It was a crystal-clear Friday night when I first walked onto the narrow gangway to board a cruise ship. Thrilled with anticipation, excitement, and wonder. What would it be like? Which way was this or that? Forward or aft? Port or starboard? Live music played harmony and variety as people danced mid-ship in the aisles and throughout the lush, carpeted atrium. Exuberance. Excitement!

Welcoming smiles awaited us as did waiters wandering with long white gloves carrying lavish platters of tempting hors d'oeuvres. Colorful frilly party toothpicks with unusual cheeses, shish kabobs, and stuffed mushroom caps sprinkled with crumbled topping, my favorite. Bubbling drinks were iridescent and created in glasses of assorted shapes and sizes along with sparkling wine decanters. I had a Seven-Up over ice served in a glass that actually lit up … like magic.

Cruising was all but a dream for me. A get-away escape. A life that I might one day enjoy. If only the chance to journey to exotic places throughout the world could come to be. Only on this night, my journey came to an end when cruise staff in picture-perfect blue blazers and smart white pants or skirts handed me packets of bright multicolored confetti.

And the clock struck ten! The ship blew a thunderous loud whistle that sounded almost musical. The signal was to disembark, get off, to go ashore. The magic was a night to remember. And, the beginning of countless dreams to eventually cruise away on a cruise ship. Later in life, that echoing horn blast sound has become my beloved part of cruising.

I grew up in Los Angeles, only miles away from The Port of Los Angeles World Cruise Center. I was in high school and then the dream date was to drive to the port on a Friday evening, board the ship and partake in the gala celebration. We danced! Tasted yummy treats! Shared festivities like no other. Walking off the ship down the gangplank was a little sad for our heads were filled with enjoyable memories and our hands were filled with overflowing confetti.

In those days security was not so tight, and visitors were encouraged to come aboard to build the anticipation, spirit, and atmosphere. Also, bio-degradable was not an issue and confetti throwing was a symbolic must. We cheered boisterously as the ship slowly left the pier as it began pushing away from the dock, sailing into the waters and out of sight. We could still hear the thunderous loud whistleblowing. The streamers of colorful confetti thrown in every direction enhanced the gaiety of the moment and fell like light rain off the ship and shore.

The first time I ever walked on a cruise ship I knew

it was only a beginning …

Really?

Those first days of teaching evolved into everyday experiences I genuinely enjoyed – to share with others and develop the positives in children. Turning 21, I remember the day I got my first paycheck. It was rewarding and, "grown-up." I now better understood/appreciated all my parents had done for me over so many years.

I deposited that first check and had the idea of doing something special for my parents. A leisure cruise? Why not? In 1970 they were barely beginning. I booked it!

My big idea created a lot of thought/planning for my parents to organize a schedule for the staff and pharmacists to cover their drug store for a whole week. I can still visualize in my mind their anticipation, planning, packing, and the specially tagged suitcases ready to go. They were off. I almost wondered who was more excited, me or them.

Today my philosophy is dedicated to "giving back" and my book, *Joyful Volunteering*, shares multiple stories on this theme. For their story, while they cruised, I was beyond happy imagining them on a ship with the freedom and total relaxation they so deserved.

When they returned from their voyage they were beaming. Nonstop story after story unfolded. (They met on a ship. That is another story, so this truly was the ultimate experience.)

A shiny prized possession held proudly in my dad's hand confused me. A trophy? They shared that they did relax although they also joined in the silly and crazy cruise games. First place! My dad won the costume contest. Interesting! (In early cruising costume evenings were as popular as formal nights.) However, they had not packed a costume in all that luggage. And so, the story goes, my jokester dad had dressed up as a pregnant woman of all things. That was not enough as he became competitive for the coveted grand trophy. When he paraded in front of the judges and cruisers watching from all levels throughout the multi-story atrium, he popped a water balloon giving the effect of his water breaking. Of all things!

Really?

How to Meet the Doctor?!

Her initial cruise! My friend Lynne always dreamed of cruising. We were off to cruise to Mexico and time for her dream to begin! She was so excited, and I was too ... to share the love of cruising with a dear friend.

We arrived at the port, checked in and the usual, walked up the gangplank to board. We wandered and explored the ship; her eyes were big just taking in the whole mood and atmosphere. We found our cabin and then the pool that looked so inviting. Waiters carried trays with colorful fancy glasses and exotic drinks. Lynne tried some though she is not usually much of a drinker. She thought they tasted delicious and actually had not eaten much that day in her excitement of finally going on a cruise.

Our happy feeling. Adventure awaiting.

I accompanied Lynne to the top deck for a view in every direction, to get a feel of the ship and the mere excitement of it all. We observed passengers gathered on deck as the celebration began. Music played and we were just about to leave the Port of Los Angeles.

As the ship gently pulled out Lynne watched the dock decreasing in size as we entered the ocean waters. The next thing she knew she was laying on the deck after I thankfully was able to break her fall. She was not hurt though embarrassed because she looked up to a group of very good-looking men. (She called them gorgeous.) They were paramedics on vacation together. Lynne wanted to go and hide though that was not even a possibility. (I was so worried.) The ship's nurse appeared with a wheelchair, and she was off to see the doctor.

To quote Lynne, "You know what they say about ship's doctors!!" He was cute and kind and did blood tests as well as giving her a chocolate candy bar. Apparently, her blood sugar and blood pressure had dropped at the same time causing her to faint. Thank goodness and then … Lynne was fine. Whew! So fine that she experienced the doctor himself walking her to the cabin. He went in and turned up the air, also tucking her in bed, and waited until she was settled and comfortable.

What an experience for a first cruise! Leave it to Lynne! All settled down and we shared a fabulous cruise. She since is now an avid world cruiser with a smile when we reflect on our adventure like no other. Lynne recalls that people called her "the lady who fainted."

She has her award-winning smile – "Knowing the adorable ship's doctor tucked me in bed on my first day of cruising."

Compliments to the Crew and More

Door Number 1 – Door Number 2 – or Door Number 3?

Walking down the halls a clearly marked door simply says, "Crew only." Only, which "crew only" door is the right one? Doors are not logically located. It takes a while. Crew gain access to different staircases and elevators to get to where they are going. On one ship (or two) we were continually lost. The halls zigzagged this way and that under the main theater. Meeting some corporate members staying for a short time onboard was reassuring to know they were lost too. In talking, we laughed that possibly dropping a trail of breadcrumbs to follow the path would be the solution!

Riding the crew elevator is a novelty. An inside elevator to take me to where I am going. Most of the crew however almost seem to fly up and down stairs to their destination. The crew areas are busy at all hours with crew members heading to and from work. I like getting in the inside crew elevator as staff from every department might be in for the ride. There is an assortment of languages spoken and crew wearing various attire. Kitchen plaids and kerchiefs, entertainer costumes, restaurant waiter vests, and dinner jackets, and more. Not too much dialogue, as all are hurrying to work. Though we cannot always communicate very well, the shared smiles and acknowledgment are what it is all about.

Drills and Regulations

Drills for the operation of watertight doors take place upon signing onto a ship and are mandatory before sailing. It is essential that crew members be familiar with systems as well as the location of a number of powered watertight doors aboard a ship. Watertight doors are special types of doors on ships that prevent the ingress of water from one compartment to another during flooding or accidents. They act as a safety barrier to stop the spread of water inside a vessel.

Each individual signing on must be checked that they have been to a drill and understand the procedures and significance. Also, keep in mind, the amount of crew maintaining the safety of everything on a cruise ship. That's what I wish – for passengers to understand there is more to crew than may be realized. Not just the positions we see them perform, but the extensive preparation. The crew are dedicated, and a training center develops and builds their many talents.

Passengers always ask where does the crew live and why are they not permitted to go in crew quarters. The workings of the ship are below passenger decks, and it is for security and the safety of the vessel. Behind the "Crew Only" areas are connected staircases and corridors and also a place where crew can feel free to relax with fellow mates from across the world. Crew areas can be full of activity when they are off as they have a chance to socialize and enjoy limited free time. The crew enjoys the gym as well as the mess hall as places to gather and discuss their day and thoughts. Life onboard offers events and activities such as karaoke, theme nights, and more. Different foods are available for various ethnic groups. There really is a "crew community."

Announcements

Once, we flew all night from Los Angeles to a foreign port and though tired, still opted we would get up early and explore the ship and possibly the port. Not! Dave and I are not late sleepers – except on that first day in crew quarters. Those announcements that we always think are too loud or too many, are not made in the crew quarters except in an emergency. Thus, it was elevenish when we realized such. We overslept! (Now we know.)

Behind the Scenes

There was one incident when as guest lecturers our cabin was located in the hallway of "staff quarters." The room steward took a few things I thought needed cleaning. To my surprise, my white pants came back as if they could walk by themselves. Perfectly pressed in the same way as the uniform of a captain. (If you can believe – looking better than when they were brand new.)

Crew members usually share a cabin with someone in their department. Often, they speak different languages, and they mostly have different work shifts. Walking past cabins often we hear laughter as well as diverse music. My favorite moment was 1 a.m. in the hallway when our next-door neighbor reappeared after performing the headliner shows of the evening. Cruising to his cabin on a unicycle! Dave's favorite moment was going through the narrow hallway to exit where the cabaret dancers were laughing, visiting, and relaxing sitting on the floor in the hallway. It was fun to see the camaraderie. Dave still tells the story of having to step over those six sets of dancer's legs stretched out in the hall.

When I first started cruising years ago, we didn't have cell phones or the technology of today. The crew would wait in long lines in a port if they were lucky enough to get off for an hour or two. If/when they got a connection, they could call home to loved ones in their home country. Now they have an internet café, and like passengers, hope for a strong signal.

The crew work every day, seven days a week: a constant day-in and day-out life onboard. Passengers cruise to relax and enjoy luxury and are spoiled each and every day. When a crew worker gets an hour or two off between shifts, they usually do not dash to shore, instead, a nap is a necessary luxury.

Before I became an Enrichment Speaker 19 years ago, I was always fascinated by the crew. To share conversation with the crew is a joy for me as I learn about their culture, beliefs, travels, and home countries. The stories about their families and lives are stories I could listen to forever. Being a speaker, it is rewarding to share knowledge and passion lecturing to educate people while exploring the world. Presentations are creative and intriguing as well as a multitude of preparation to lecture to audiences of every age from all walks of life.

I often bring t-shirts and hats from California. The crew have limited funds of which most are sent home. (And, no time to shop.) To wear a new t-shirt is a gift of choice. The smile of a crew member going to the crew bar late at night in something new and different is significant. You know, the feeling of wearing something new!

Every cruise has a hardworking crew, making sure that every voyage is smooth sailing. The crew goes the extra mile and often grow within a company. Years ago, we met Isabela, a gal from Romania, who spoke little to no English. She shared smiles and merely checked your name on the dining diagram as you were seated for dinner in the main dining room. Upon later returning to the cruise line, she was higher up in her role in the dining room. And on a third return, she spoke seemingly perfect English and was working in the excursion desk. It was special when we cruised to Egypt to share stories with her. We talked about ancient Egypt and civilization and of course, our visit to the pyramids. We bought a stuffed camel that makes unusual noises, one for her and one for us. And the last time we saw Isabela, she was the head of excursions, was blonde instead of brunette, and spoke five or more languages fluently as passengers prepared for excursions and explorations.

First Impressions

One day off the cruise ship to encounter Jamaica – I remember wandering at the falls at Dunns River, tasting jerk chicken, sipping Mountain Blue coffee while viewing the lovely Caribbean Sea, and hearing an unknown language spoken so fast.

"There's a course for every player." Jamaica's sweeping landscapes, magnificent vistas, and distinctive golf courses were the descriptions, so I made a reservation to try my hand at golf. Runaway Bay was enticing as a "natural beautiful place" on the island. I met the caddy who seemed approachable and interested until he realized I am left-handed. He questionably gave me pointers on stance and the holding of the club. I listened and the vast greens and picturesque setting were encouraging. And so it began, I thought maybe a little promising, until I looked up from the struggle of how to hold the club and swing to see a live bull roaring my way. There really was no escape, so I was told to run, zigzag, and disrupt the bull. That is all I remember, I did … run away!

To conclude about the first time I went to Jamaica, I felt such hustle and hassle and actually, annoyance. Not what I anticipated nor a place I would dream of returning to in the future. All the ads and in the movies, "One Love – Come to Jamaica." Not!

However, on the flight home, others were teary that they had to leave Jamaica. So, out of curiosity about what I missed, I called the airline not too long after and there were a few seats available for the date I wanted to return. So, I booked it!

On my first day upon my curious return to Jamaica, I checked into an all-inclusive for a week to have a chance for a complete experience. I got into the Jacuzzi that bubbled and felt a soothing mist while sitting amidst other vacationers. I was starting to soak in the hot whirlpool, feeling the jets, beginning to relax, and listening to the others socializing about this and that. I felt a little sprinkle and before I knew it, pouring rain. (Note – this was my trial return to Jamaica and so far, I had only been there a very short time.) Some of the vacationers began to express negatives and what to do in the rain as the attendant came over with the largest smile. "No problem." And with that, he handed me a "Purple Rain." Stunning purple color and it was as delicious as it looked. (Blended ice and fresh fruit, grenadine for color, and blue curacao … with a little paper umbrella.) I had read that "Irie" means "everything is alright and fine." And I knew then, Jamaica … was going to be Irie!

No problem! (As they say in Jamaica.) I had returned with an open mind and … Jamaica became my favorite place to be! Yes, the beauty of it all. Powdery white-sand beaches, walking along the river's edge, floating on a raft, and even the craft markets. I think it is the rhythm of the land. Most attractive to me is the warmth of the people. I immersed myself into the Jamaica that others crave, and I appreciated the vibrant culture, incredible music, and folklore shared by the locals. My favorite is the conch soup, even on a hot day, as I experienced a breeze in the air and reggae music in the background. Perfect! First impressions for me were – wrong. So much so, that I have returned countless times to various parts of Jamaica and now cannot help to love the Jamaican culture.

I looked into teaching at a university in Jamaica. Ahh – life on an island filled with reggae music and international influence. Michael was young at the time, and I made the decision to visit Jamaica when possible and keep our roots in California.

I try to share stories of my multiple happenings, experiences, and visits to Jamaica with others. So, in writing this book, I hear in my mind the reggae beat and reveal my love of Jamaica. Unforgettable!

Sometimes Jamaica is hot … tropical … and humid too. What to do with your hair? Plus, how to look nice on special cruise nights? There is an easy way to have a cool and fun, different look. And guys, even with little to no hair, you can have a braid or two or three too! It's your vacation!

Decisions! 54 braids and counting. What color for the beads? What style? Where to place the part and braids?

Cornrows. When getting braided – famous words to clearly say … not too tight! Each braid is an intricate form or pattern created by interlacing material such as ribbons or yarns and colorful beads at the end to se-cure each braid. The secret to undoing the cornrows … A lot of conditioners so the hair will not pull nor hurt.

It is fun to return home with the new hairdo. A lot of attention. People come up and it is enjoyable to share stories and encourage travel and the world. Living in Southern California, I prefer Jamaica over Hawaii. Yes, Hawaii is beautiful and inspiring and a place like no other. The same number of hours on the plane, yet Jamaica has its own vibe! The music, food, and culture are that of another country. The language is spoken fast and almost sounds like a Pig Latin some of us attempted when young. I bought a book with vo-cabulary and hints on speaking Patois and have prac-ticed though I think I sound comedic.

Aaaaaarrrrrgh! Known for pirates, Jamaica has a wicked history. Popular trade routes over years brought pirates including the legendary Sir Henry Morgan. I may have met you on a Caribbean voyage, I share guest lectures on Pirates. Even, one whole talk entitled "Women Pirates – The Most Dangerous of Them All." And, I reveal the true meaning of Aaaaaarr-rrrgh!

Buying souvenirs – the word is a French word meaning tribute or memory. A token to bring a touch home as a taste or tribute to a destination or travels. We all have our own tastes for momentos or artifacts. "White Witch," my favorite, is described as a citrus-spicy scent they say represents powers and legends from Jamaica. ("Timeless magic if you dare.") To me, it is a flowery and light cologne fragrance.

A Rastafarian day was a cruise tour that seemed like a must for Dave and me on one Jamaica visit. The shuttle took us over windy roads and through amazing hills. We walked through a flowing stream to reach the village of our destination. The members of the Rastafarian community live a life in and of nature. They welcomed us to better recognize and participate in their way of life. We rotated to various stations including art, handicrafts, carving, music, gardening, singing, health, nature, and food. The final lesson was in creating a hot chocolate drink from fresh cocoa beans. We took turns stirring over the hot open fire. I was warm and asked for some water to quench my thirst. Refreshing, it was served in a handmade cup that was half of a coconut shell. (Reusable and contributing to saving the planet.) Lunch included freshly picked steamed vegetables that were juicy yet crisp with an idea about cultivation and natural ingredients.

In another country or city or wherever you go, interacting with the locals tells you more about a place than anything. You can read pamphlets and books, take a tour, shop, yet time with a local says volumes. A day with the Rastafari people was an opening to healthy living and connectedness with nature. Beating their handmade drums of great sounds had rhythm and tradition, and the technique demonstrated of the art of carving, and more was inspiring. A cross-cultural exchange paves a way to awareness and a better understanding of others and ourselves too.

Hair braiding is more than a hustle, it is a happening! No worries, in the Caribbean and tropical ports, people will find you to ask if you want braiding. It is a talent, an art. Sitting there on a low stool often crooked and wooden, having the weave of braids placed into your hair brings a closeness. Each visit I have done this, mostly to meet and interact with locals. I have learned more in those moments than in any studies. A time to hear of others about their village, life, personal family story, and history, to hear a tune, and just delve into the life of others. I have met children, grandchildren, parents, cousins, dogs, cats, parrots, and even pet goats.

At the conclusion of a cruise, passengers give thought to highlights and special moments of the voyage. It has been rewarding to me, more than once, when someone came up to me to say that inspiring them to get cornrows was a trip highlight. Something as simple as braids have created comfort, global awareness, and possibly a deeper understanding of people wherever we may go.

Bye, Bye!

Know that the ship could/will leave without you!
Listen to those tips about being on time and when the
ship will be sailing. They do sail without you! Ships
are on a tight schedule, so it is essential to leave on
time to get to the next port on time. (Leaving late
means having to make up time which uses a lot of ex-
pensive fuel. And, once they are moving, they cannot
turn around and come back.) I remember years ago I
often wandered and explored ports on my own. Somehow though, maybe I was just lucky. I haven't missed
the ship yet!

Did you hear that loudspeaker asking so and so to
contact the purser at once? It is not someone famous
nor the winner of a contest, it is who never made it
back to the ship.

One friend, Jim, was intrigued with the locals in
Russia and lost track of time. (Of all places.) He arrived
after his name was called saying, "Contact the purser
at once!" As the ship was within minutes of sailing, his
one foot after the other barely stepped onto the gangplank … just in time. Whew!

I have watched crowds out on deck wave to a taxi
scurrying through the gate into the cruise terminal as

we were already sailing out to sea.

Mind your time on the daily newsletter and possibly a note on your pillow the night before. If it says to set your watch ahead or backward, there is a reason. I can't tell you how many passengers enthralled with an exciting beach or shopping excursion have been sorry.

Once in Morocco, we were told to stay on ship time as their time was different. That caused confusion and lost souls. (Actually, the same thing happened in Gibraltar.) Part of traveling is awareness – paying attention.

Only if you book an excursion with the ship, will they wait for you. In Mexico, a day full of snorkeling and a lavish buffet was memorable. I loved gliding on an inner tube in the immense ocean. Somehow the catamaran to bring us back was sluggish and our watches knew it. The ship waited for us knowing that the tour was delayed.

A "Hop on – Hop off" bus in Copenhagen was an ideal way to visit the city with different choices of sightseeing routes and attractions. Many cruisers choose this flexible form of exploring with an open ticket valid for twenty-four hours. They advertise, "Hear and discover surprising things about our city." Nevertheless, when it actually came time to "Hop-on" … the large double-decker buses have a maximum capacity of persons to safely be onboard. Surprise? Even on that type of adventure, you might have to wait for another bus as there are only so many making the circle. Allow extra time.

Ahh – the oompah music in a festive procession of costumes, large balloons, cartwheels, and song in a foreign language. Dancers in the streets with a merry-making celebration of festivity amidst street barriers that guide the fascinating parade. Lavish celebration, so much so that more than a few cruisers could not obtain a way to return to the departing ship.

So, there are pros and cons of flexible, on your own, exploration to enhance port days in unique destinations. I like to opt as I go and often find the great taste of local food or ultimate discovery in a native village. Mistakes happen, despite best-laid plans; you can find yourself still on dry land while your ship is sailing off.

Talking to some who have found themselves stranded, they say formulate a game plan, and you might even explore a destination or an out-of-the-way place. Vehicles break down, parades come to town, traffic jams happen, and passengers need to take heed, so they don't miss out on anything. Especially missing the ship!

"Can't find the ship!" Cruise ships are pretty big to lose. Once I when I was cruising, the weather conditions changed. The captain needed to take the ship out sooner than scheduled for safety reasons. Somehow through walkie-talkies and phones, excursions booked onboard ship were hurried back in time. All but one. Can you imagine returning from a tour and not seeing your ship? The tour returned with participants wondering, "Where oh where can the ship be?" Because they were on a ship tour, the staff arranged for them to take a speed boat and catch up. What a scare ... and ... what an adventure they had!

I do have a secret about traveling. Crave adventure, journey to a new destination, find picturesque sightseeing, and imagine the excitement no matter what the language is.

My dad taught me! He said to ask a cab driver, "How is the weather today?" as I look at my wrist. If the reply tells me the time, I know that the driver telling me, "I speak English," does not.

Serendipity

St. Kitts seemed to be calling me. Saint Kitts and Nevis is a dual-island nation located between the Atlantic Ocean and the Caribbean Sea. My memory was of high peaks, lush and tropical, an imposing volcano, the beauty of hearing creole spoken, and a soothing sea breeze. I was so excited that on this cruise I would be returning to breathtaking St. Kitts.

The islands have almost a sibling rivalry, though both are equally spectacular in my memory. Lush trees and astounding blue waters with relaxing white-sand beaches. I was thinking about taking a tour to visit the Brimstone Hill Fortress with a view from atop Timothy Hill revealing the Atlantic Ocean and the Caribbean Sea. Also, there is the Romney Manor with tropical gardens and the Caribelle Batik Factory celebrating history and creativity.

I connected with a tour company that sounded low-key and interesting. In the past when there my feet had touched the soft sand and the refreshing crystal-clear waters were perfect for that relaxing holiday. Done! A tour was now planned, speeches ready and I just could not wait to return to the islands.

And then ... one night ... I received an intriguing

email. The owners of the recommended tour company included Krista, a dedicated educator with a serendipitous thought. "I know this is a rather strange question, however, could you please contact me about speaking on the island." She had my name, she looked up my bio and was determined. Interesting? I said ... Yes.

The ship sailed and the cruise was enjoyable up until I got off the ship in St. Kitts. The highlight! I walked the boardwalk and there before me was a cheerful smile on Krista holding a distinctive welcome Gail sign. I "worked" on the island and the day I will cherish. I visited the local school; I spoke in a large hall to uniformed children of different ages. My lecture was hands-on, and the participants picked from the audience were eager to join in. I gave a talk to the local educators on motivation and the positives of reaching each and every child. After, the interaction of questions and conversation was rewarding. And then, my final talk was to island educators and even to members of the ministry of education. This was an opportunity to share my philosophy of *Joyful Learning.* (The title of my first book.)

One never knows. All I did was plan a tour ... and I received the greatest trip around the island even imaginable. Krista took me here, there, and everywhere. Her generosity and enthusiasm made it a perfect day. (Unfortunately, I knew I had to return to the ship although I did return to St. Kitts another year and of course visited Krista and her adorable daughter.)

I must share about the population of St. Kitts, more

monkeys than people? That is what they say. Ver-
vet monkeys from Africa. The island land was once
dominated by sugarcane plantations and the animals
became hooked on the alcohol in fermented sugarcane
juice left out in the fields. Monkeys seem to be everywhere and are playful, mischievous, and naughty. I
can only laugh as I share this memory. The expression
"If you snooze, you lose" applies here. These creatures
are in reality very choosy as to what they long for.
They are cute with a quest! Some will actually tip a
beverage of a sleeping beachgoer to determine if the
drink is with alcohol or without. Most crave and love
to sip their spirits, while others prefer not. To put it
nicely, there are the binge drinkers and the sober ones,
as some monkeys scurry around and some ... tipsy ...
just fall down. (I had a Zing, the refreshing non-alco-
holic local orange soda pop drink at a spectacular bay
... they did not bother me.) I guess you call it "monkey
business."

What can top those monkeys on a day like no other?
Leave it to my guide! We drove through spectacular
scenery this way and that to the top of a mountain.
You could see the ship as the intimate restaurant faced
it, though this all seemed unbelievable. The restaurant was noted for entertaining royalty such as Princess Diana and others. Fine dining overlooking the
harbor and masterfully prepared cuisine was artfully
arranged with fresh-picked herbs from the garden, locally caught fish, and all so delicious.

Indescribable. My thoughts swirled with the fulfillment of presenting in this Caribbean country and

before leaving the surroundings and the scenic mountain I had to pause to snap a picture. For the name of the charming island restaurant was – Serendipity.

The Itsy-Bitsy Bikini Story

There is shopping – and there is shopping! For the quest of the ideal bathing suit!

And so, it goes – I am not a shopper, yet I did it – I shopped for my turquoise blue bikini. I actually liked the fit as well as the aqua color, like the ocean. I wore it on my cruise to begin my tan, to enjoy the beach, and for a dip in the Jacuzzi. The hot tub is up on the top deck with lots to reflect on, people, the view, and the journey. Ahhh – leisure.

I returned to the cabin so very relaxed ready to shower and dress for dinner. I always put my wet bathing suit in a towel and ask Dave to stomp on it. This takes out some of the moisture for a faster dry. Usually, I next hang it up to fully dry. This always works like a charm. We dressed colorfully for "Caribbean Night" and dashed off to enjoy music, dinner, and an entertaining cruise evening.

It was the very next day when I suddenly came to a realization that unsettled me. I realized that the towel with my bikini was nowhere to be found! The room steward took it not knowing and uh-oh – one new bikini I so loved … missing.

What to do? Obviously, it had gone rolled in a thick

terry towel to the ship laundry. Of all things for a little bikini. The staff, upon my inquiry, directed me to the purser to check lost and found. Oh no! Now I had to go to the purser's desk to discuss my lost little bikini.

Then there were the forms! I was given page upon page and told to carefully fill out every single detail to include all of the required information. You would think I lost a diamond ring. A lot for a tiny bikini! Description. When last seen. Value. And, more … So, I finished each and every line on those long-printed forms. Whew! Upon completion, I was given quite a look when I was told two completed reports were required – as two pieces had been lost.

Days went by and it was a frustrating and almost a forgotten incident. So, is that my sad itsy-bitsy bikini story? Almost all hope was gone.

And then – in the cabin on the last afternoon packing while reminiscing about the cruise – there was a knock, knock at the door. Through the peephole, I could not believe my eyes. There was a uniformed officer. Lots went through my mind … I slowly opened the door. The officer appeared looking a bit embarrassed holding a clipboard of paperwork. And, on a hangar, dangled the perfectly pressed itsy-bitsy bikini!

An Ichiban Voyage

The puffy clouds were low, I noticed the crew spoke no English, and I observed the cars drive onto a ferry boat. Japan is home to a network of many islands. There are many styles of "cruising." Remarkable for me was going on that ferry across a bay while watching spewing ashes and smoke coming into view. Cruising on an open ferry in Japan was an experience. It was my first time in southern Japan, and I felt honored to be there as a recipient being an American Fulbright Memorial Scholar.

The area of Kyushu is best known for Sakurajima, an active volcano that faces Kinko Bay. Interesting, the force of mother nature. I spotted species of animals, forests, plants, and more in their natural state. The ferry moved towards lands and islands beyond even in my dreams.

The ferry ride landed me in Kagoshima, the seaside city on Japan's Kyushu Island and the capital of Kagoshima Prefecture. While in Kagoshima I was paired to be with a family to better understand Japanese life. Masami Yamamoto's family was the best! She shared with me her love of laughter, cooking, and walking on the beach. Many traditions were discussed and shared.

So far away across the world and yet so close in finding ways to communicate.

Japan is a long, thin island country with the Pacific Ocean on one side and the Sea of Japan and East China Sea on the other. The length of the country finds an extensive coastline with lots of beaches. Some were more sparsely populated than others though the ambiance of any beach is fulfilling. The roll of the waves, the texture of the sand, and breathing in of our senses.

For hundreds of years, the Japanese have traveled to the shore for a sandy cure of many ailments. While there, I had my first-time sand bathing (**sun-amushi**) in Ibusuki. This involved **putting on a yukata and** being covered in hot black sand, actually very warm to the touch. Supposedly the volcanic steam transfers from the sand to the body. For comfort, a towel was fixed around my neck to avert the grainy substance from getting into my face. Laying in that hot ... hot sand, for me, was more than I could endure for very long. Being in southernmost Japan, challenged my geography as I roasted in the sizzling sand while realizing the location and gazing at the world around me.

I explored different beaches, coming home with sand in my shoes and, ... we all have an uh-oh moment at some time when traveling. I sure did! Always, leave the shoes outside of the home in Japan. Of course! Only one day, the kindness of meeting the neighbors in a welcoming community, I ran back to go inside and get my camera to capture the moments. In the excitement, I forgot to take off my shoes, and the faces and reactions were more than I want to remember.

I knew I would take other ferry boats to more tastes of Japan. I wanted to experience as much of the southern part of Japan while there. I had the chance to visit where they grow sweet potatoes for pie, candy, and vegetables. It is also the main ingredient to make shochu, a strong liquor spirit.

Pizza in Japan? Of course. Maybe, the most fascinating of all pizza with a unique spin is called Okonomiyaki. Say that word fast! Twice?! It Sizzles on a grill, is shaped round, and has a consistency of a wheat flour batter with egg, shredded cabbage, and cook's choice. The texture is more like a sizable pancake. A sauce is placed on top with other ingredients, usually healthy veggies.

Buy your ticket for another kind of "boat" journey and ride in an amusement park at The Water Garden Park. This was high-speed and a spinning rush through flowing waters. Only it was noodles swirling round and round and round. (I always thought this could be a novelty in the states.) Running water noodles! I visualized in my mind the I Love Lucy episode of mishaps when she worked in the chocolate factory, as this staff couldn't keep up with those noodles! Noodles raced in the water and eventually, you used your chopsticks to grab your noodles. (Warning if you are hungry, it takes many attempts to get your food as noodles spin rapidly.) And, did your parents ever tell you, "Never play with food!" So, fun!

Riding the ferry transported me into a better awareness of a foreign place, eyeing in every direction.

Scenic splendor … of which way to look first? Ocean on one side and green pines growing from lava. Natural beauty and stunning views enveloped scenery and a taste of the culture of Japan. The opportunity of immersing in a different culture increased my understanding of the world around me.

Some years later I was speaking at an educational conference in Hawaii. Michael traveled with me for a Hawaiian experience and some time together. We flew from Los Angeles to Oahu in a five-hour flight, plus had an adjustment to the time difference, and finally, tiredly walked into the lobby of our hotel. There in the lobby, seated on a couch, was my "Japanese family" who flew to Hawaii to surprise me. What a feeling! I could not believe my eyes! Oh, they were thrilled to meet an American teenager, Michael. We walked a few blocks to a buffet of every food imaginable; Western, Hawaiian, and shared tastes and dialogue.

I have kept in touch since with Masami and the family. After cruising to Japan a few years ago, arriving in Tokyo, across a courtyard I heard a familiar voice, "Gail … Gail …" Now Dave had a chance to meet my "family" and we spent our days together, glorious, exploring Japan getting an inside view of this fabulous country. It was the best experience and as they say in Japan … Ichiban!

As I write this, recalling my ferry boat ride, I would not want to be on it today. News reports the high plumes of smoke are billowing from an active volcano. "Sakurajima shot smoke and ash miles into the sky." I just wish everyone safe.

Not a Sombrero

A colorful day in Mexico on a glorious scenic beach with vast sands and clear blue waters. The vibes were relaxed, and I heard the strumming of a guitar in the background. Locals came by selling trinkets, hammocks, blankets, jewelry, local crafts, cold drinks, tortillas, sombreros, and other assorted hats stacked tall.

Relaxed and working on my tan, I welcome the vendors and their stories and smiles. I like to buy something as they stroll miles of beaches in that hot sun with limited sales and profit. I bought a watermelon fruit ice cream bar which was tasty though it softened and melted so quickly. On this day I also bought a funny frog hat that caught my eye. It was brilliant bright green made of a felt-like soft material. It reminded me of the Statue of Liberty hats sold in New York. It was useless for keeping the sizzling sun off of my face.

Somehow, I am always thinking ahead and so a thought crossed my mind. I was on vacation from teaching a multi-aged group of elementary children and we always are having thematic studies.

Frogs? Nature? Leaping? Habitat? I could visualize it all before me. What a possibly perfect costume for a unique scientific study and presentation. Frog hats?!

I walked across the hot sand to a walkway. I proudly held the hat that I thought could bring possibilities.

My Spanish is unfortunately limited though I can usually get by. Before I knew it, I bargained with a vendor and began purchasing frog hats. As many as possible! So, there I was with a smile, tan, and determination holding stacks of frog hats. (I reflected on a monkey and cap seller story that all children love.) Only it was me! Passersby surrounded me to purchase … frog hats. What had I done?

When I returned to the ship, I was a sight to be seen. I got some curious looks. On vacation, anything can be. Who else would buy 31 vivid bright green frog hats with a bright red tongue and bulging white eyes?

I would pack them up when I would disembark and bring my brilliant discovery to school. I placed them on the small table in the corner of the cabin and all was forgotten. Not!

In the middle of the night, my loving Mom woke up to a shocking and disturbing discovery. For there in the corner of our cabin were eyeballs all staring at her. Lots of them! Florescent like and shiny bright. 31 frogs, times two mighty glowing eyeballs each = 62 eyes staring unexpectedly at Mom.

Never a dull moment in travel. Another non-stop laugh and the frogs? They were a successful sensation at a science presentation unlike no other. Imagine what children looked like with eyes bright jumping with delight in their frog hats.

About a Big Rock, Something Cute & a Very Unqualified Driver

One of the most surprising experiences happened on a cruise that stopped in Gibraltar. You had to see it to believe it. The famous Rock of Gibraltar is a high limestone rock rising out of the sea. Soaring up on the hill, a unique location, the panorama of Spain and Africa, an incredible view, all in one sight. It is amazing to look out in the distance to be on one continent and see another.

Gibraltar has an "old city" plus a fishing village and a meandering main street. On a seemingly ideal day, I unexpectedly endured a deluge of rain and scurried for refuge. I literally stumbled into one of the pubs for shelter. Old pubs line narrow roads with history as well as fish and chips, lager and ale. Gibraltarians shared a strong sense of unity and locals were welcoming to share history and song.

Feeling the wonder of travel, I next entered the stunning St. Michael's cave to view the magical spectacular stalactites and stalagmites. Coming out is damp and slippery so we walked carefully in the midst and moisture. As we approached the van we had to glance twice. We could not believe our eyes. Monkeys were looking through the telescopes at the scenic view stop, emulating the tourists. "The Rock" has wild monkeys roaming who seem intelligent and might steal your belongings (lunch/hat) if you stop to marvel at the natural environment or take a photo.

To our surprise, Barbary macaque monkeys had actually climbed in through the sunroof of the van. One was in the back seat as if impatiently waiting for the tour to continue and the other, carefully observing us and sitting in the driver's seat honking and holding onto the steering wheel. Eventually to our relief, they scampered out the door to amuse and harass other tourists.

A Safe Story

I always saved some money, so a mother-daughter cruise was possible. We booked a "run of ship" guarantee. Perfect, as we wanted the lowest rate possible and the guarantee of a cabin – somewhere? (Often an upgrade from "somewhere" we were told might even be possible?) We arrived at the port and received our cabin assignment. Embarkation day had begun. Happy just to have the time to be traveling together, it was an inside cabin, perfectly fine, and we felt we wouldn't be spending that much time in the cabin anyway.

We took a little time to unwind and unpacked to get that over with before the movement of the ship sailing. So, we were settled in and looked forward to sharing our new adventure. We were handed a map so next; we roamed the ship from bow to stern to navigate and see what we could see. We went to the mandatory muster drill and accessed the top deck to look at the view.

Acclimated to ship life, it becomes a home away from home. The first morning we had my favorite, room service in our stateroom, a lazy way to begin and a luxury amenity. Why not? The first day was a sea day, a day in transit, and the perfect time to make the most of the ship. Mom visited the ship's library and found a quiet corner to read her new book while I found a lounge out on deck to listen to live calypso music and get some sunshine.

There was a myriad of activities, and we always left each other notes of where we would be and when. We reassembled late in the day in time to get ready for the evening dinner and show. We were introduced to interesting dining companions and shared a leisurely indulgent multiple course dinner. They ordered an array of desserts too as encouraged by the waiter. Gooey, multi-layered decadent, and ornamental-colored sweets endlessly continued to arrive at our table. (Mom always said her secret to reaching into her nineties was her passion for chocolate so she was pleased and, no, remarkably happy.) Growing up we always laughed at a mom so loving sweets and a daughter not.

Since that would be our assigned dining table for each night, I quietly whispered to the waiter that I am not so into desserts as I am into healthy vegetables. I must tell you that when we strolled into the dining room the second night, one table stood out with an enormous indescribable spectacular floral-style bouquet. When we finally found our table with the sign number 57, the masterpiece was our centerpiece. Indeed! The bouquet was the most original and creative vegetable garden imaginable. With a design similar to a color wheel, were artistically cut flower buds of different sizes and heights made of edible veggies. My wish came true! It was tasty and we actually met so many fellow cruisers as they stopped by to photograph our table. (A problem for the maître d' – the next night several other tables, of course, asked for the same.)

The headline production show in the theater was a "must-see" and was extravagant and enjoyable. All in all, a great beginning of a voyage. We found our way back to our cabin and truthfully, we were two tired cruisers.

When we lazily woke up on day three there was a note under our door. It read that a mistake had been made and our cabin was intended to be, indeed, an upgrade. Always something! We were packed and moved to a top deck and a beautiful, upgraded window-perfect cabin. A remarkable treat from the uncertain "run of ship" guarantee. And so, as the voyage continued, there were so many special unforgettable marvelous moments that Mom and I shared together.

Our cruise was unforgettable! All good things they say must come to an end and thus – we had to pack for the disembark. To our disappointment, we did not have the keys to Mom's condo for our return to Los Angeles. Of all things! We realized that in the move to an upgrade they had been left in the safe. The crew questioned the couple who had been reassigned to our former cabin and they claimed to know – nothing. (Obviously, somehow, something seemed amiss.) We went ashore and proceeded to the van to the airport to homeward bound. Landing close to midnight a cab whisked us to her residence and a locksmith was called. To this day though, a cruise tip, always swipe your hand all across the bottom of your in-cabin safe to be sure nothing is left behind. That was not the way to end a perfect trip – but what can you do? So, with smiles, we just focused on the wonderful memories of our trip.

A Fountain of Champagne

There is a mystery in how 666 champagne glasses stack together to make a glistening, flowing, waterfall glass fountain. Occasionally, I like to go early on and watch the step-by-step building of the tower. If you try this at home, I was told of the in-the-know tips: All glasses to be exactly the same size, obviously a sturdy table for the base of the construction, the tower to get successively smaller as the tower rises layer by layer. And, most of all, patience! One champagne glass upon another and the cascade of flowing champagne and bubbling is an impressive sight to see.

The union of passengers usually on the next to the last cruise night is a connection like none other. Pouring the bubbly is exciting as people surrounding you and throughout the atrium watch. Waitstaff circulate so that participants each have a glass in hand. Passengers and crew represent all walks of life and nations across the globe as glasses are raised and a toast is made. When one looks up and observes the many levels of the dramatic staircase, one also notices the faces and smiles.

Passengers from around the world choose to wear their evening best. Some women are in gowns and others in dresses, beautiful sarees, or traditional ki-monos, while men look handsome whether in suits, tuxedos, or kilts. (A kilt is symbolic and often gets a second glance and attention.) Passengers on a voyage share a journey sailing the high seas. Though we can hear the countless different languages, there is a shared experience and one unified toast and cheer. And as I look around, I always wonder why the world can't be like that?

Seven Layers

Squished, squashed, smashed into seven layers ...

I was always curious about globes. I wanted to go see the world! My desire to see all seven continents became – reality! I was speaking on a cruise ship in South America when offered the opportunity to fly to Antarctica. It took me one second to say ... Yes!

A California girl with the warmest of clothes. Not! Word got out quickly though. I did not know the passengers who knocked on my cabin door to loan me clothes. I put on seven layers, two wool hats, two pairs of gloves, men's boots over my boots, and ... felt like a stuffed sausage. None of this would have ever been possible without ... fellow cruisers. It seemed like they were as enthusiastic as I was.

In the next incredibly early morning, I was bundled in cozy layers and on my way to Antarctica. People reaching out and giving in their small way was to me a giant gesture that taught me so much ... that dreams can come true.

I exited the cruise ship and boarded a surprisingly small plane with veterinarian, Betsy Pincheira, who is a scientist and wildlife expert. What a view! Clouds. Shadows. Ice. Almost, like floating over powdery enormous marshmallows and limitless waters. (When the plane was approaching landing, I overheard the captain say it was not always possible with the storminess of the seas plus the lack of visibility and varied weather circumstances.) I was there among Chilean, Russian, and German scientists. I kept thinking, so why can't the world get along? I could barely walk and waddled ... just like a penguin.

A remarkable continent! Antarctica gave me an up-close look at stunning birds that most of us only read about. Their flippers are like propellers instead of wings and are covered with tiny stiff feathers. Some penguins were swimming in from the sea with effortless swift movement through the waters. Females making their way back from the distant sea where she nourished herself to bring food back for the newborn chick. Males remained together for warmth and were stationary protecting the eggs and offspring.

Cold arctic winds like I have never imagined nor experienced. I will never forget going ashore paddling in icy waters in a tiny zodiac to arrive at a penguin colony of loud creatures shuffling around in their own habitat and world. I became too confident when I made the miscalculation of opening my outer jacket. The wild blowing fierce wind running through me about blew me down with a blast of intensely cold air.

All of my senses heightened navigating the beauty of land unusual with wildlife of nature surrounding me. Thousands of miles away from everything, words cannot describe the peaceful serenity and emotions.

The day I was there was like the "March of the

Penguins." Heartwarming. I captured the yearly extraordinary journey of the process of penguins leaving the ocean to march inland. The remarkable love and bonding as penguins returned to reunite with their mate and family.

I witnessed astounding scenery, wildlife, and penguins. Trying to understand their harsh life and family dedication, how fortunate was I to be there up close with the remarkable creatures. I was told, "Penguins have the right of way."

The penguins curiously encountered me, a human, and snubbed (ignored) me as I stood there frozen and fascinated. Glistening formal-like tuxedos. (Like on gala formal night?) They have webbed feet and cannot walk well so they just shuffled and waddled all around me. The vast land looked to me like what I think space might look like. It was like a foreign land – the land of penguins.

A Trophy and a Triumph

Dave and I were lecturing on a ship appreciating the audience and interaction. Some people recognized me from the Scripps National Spelling Bee. I had mentored a young contestant who spelled all the way to the final day of the competition. (Tied for 14th.) Quite an accomplishment.

The Scripps National Spelling Bee is an annual academic competition since 1925. (Also called "The Super Bowl of Spelling.") Competitors request the root's language of origin and definition to help provide a clue for the correct spelling. (Try "schwarmerel.") The bee encourages and enriches vocabularies while widening knowledge of the English language. A misspelling is an elimination. The next speller then gets a new word. All striving to be the champion, contestants are from all 50 states, several territories, and other English-speaking countries.

Kendra Yoshinaga and I co-authored *The Spelling Bee and Me: A Real-Life Adventure in Learning*. Dave was the illustrator. Our book documents the real-life story of inside moments before and during the Washington D.C. spelling bee from a youth's viewpoint along with tips for future spelling mentors.

Once we were asked if we could present a – "Spelling Bee at Sea." The thought sounded unique and exciting. Dozens of passengers signed up for participation in the "Spelling Bee at Sea." These are a few of the Scripps words: auslaut; erysipelas; bougainvillea; aiguillette; pendeloque; smaragdine; cernuous; esquamulose. For our contest we made up a list for the "Spelling Bee at Sea" and it was a fun and challenging experience for all involved. An example of our "sea" related words: circumnavigation; traveled; dinghy; helm; excursion; nautical; anchor; foreign; embark; peregrination; vessel; amenities; bridge; seafaring; landlubber; muster.

The audience was silent, and the competition began! Spelling the words seemed significant though the rivalry was all in fun. Contestants asked for definitions and pronunciations. Dave, who was the illustrator for my *Spelling Bee and Me* book, drew at a large easel and guided the audience to draw with him. When a word was misspelled, the contestant left the stage. Round one, round two, round three … and … eventually the champion triumphed. Cheers and smiles and why not, something different to do on a cruise ship.

The champion who defeated all the opponents was beyond ecstatic. The woman was so thrilled as we awarded her the trophy that she proudly held up high for all to see. And so, it was, a successful one and only "Spelling Bee at Sea."

Every voyage contains that special moment and memory – often one that you least expect. On the day of disembarkation, there is always confusion and also emotion as passengers walk down that gangplank one final time. The spelling champion smiling ear to ear found us at the last of moments. That was when we truly learned the success of our spelling bee! For you see (choked up as I think about it), she explained that the reason she came on the cruise, alone, was because doctors gave her a short window of life with a prevailing illness. She came against odds and some not understanding her. Success! She was going home with a trophy and a story of triumph to share.

A Sweet Fortune

Midnight. Merry-making. Celebrate the beginning of the new year. May your wishes come true! It was a New Year's cruise and how exciting to share the moments in my Enrichment talks. My audience and I reflected upon the last year while looking ahead to the future's possibilities. We all seemed to be taking small steps towards creating a positive approach to life in the new year. I included resolutions and my stories that I had featured in *Chicken Soup for the Soul* books.

I like fortune cookies, yet on my visits to China, I was never given a fortune cookie. The best part for me is the paper inside which I look for. Fortune cookie messages can be wishful, inspiring, and at times laughable.

I introduced fortune cookies in my presentation. Passengers had fun sharing individual fortunes and messages. The little paper messages from within the cookies went out of the room with hope and wonder.

This created a fun dialogue around the ship. The new year had begun!

Sometime later I received a touch of something fortunate to me personally. It was a message from a passenger with thought and reflection and an unexpected "fortune."

Hello Gail and Dave,

I hope all is well in your part of the world and that you and your family are now home. I have to share something with you Gail that will make you smile.

Onboard the ship in one of our groups you gave us fortune cookies. I kept the motto inside mine and it also had six numbers. I put those numbers on the lottery and last week won ten pounds! I used those ten pounds and bought a beautiful bouquet for a lady I was about to visit. She had been through a tremendously bad time lately and her face was an absolute picture of joy when she received them.

It's a nice story don't you think?
Once again, every happiness to you.

Where Oh Where Has Rick Gone?

Jan Jewel wrote this who sadly has passed away ...

As she was ill, I was mostly in denial only with so much hope. Her dream was to travel with me, the two of us, on an exotic cruise adventure. Sadly, this did not happen in her lifetime. However, she gave me an elegant sparkly black scarf with streaks of silver and gold throughout. I took it with me first to Argentina and on trips thereafter. Jan is with me on many voyages.

My husband who can eat anyone under the table and never gain weight could not wait to get on the cruise ship. All the food you want to eat ... all the time. Cruising is the only time I do not hear, "I'm hungry." Breakfast buffets, lunch buffets, snacks, and sit-down dinners are the things Rick looks most forward to in cruising. We had been already on three cruises and this time we were going with friends.

I lost my husband! It was on the third day into our Panama Canal Cruise. It was just about five o'clock in the afternoon and he was nowhere to be found. To tell you the truth, this went on for about three or four days and at the same exact time, each day. All he would say to me is, "I'll be back."

Usually, at that time, I would start to get ready for dinner and a gala evening on a cruise ship. I did not really miss him the first few days that it happened. Well, I was a little ... suspicious. So, finally, on the fourth day, I decided to go looking for him. I took a walk around the ship. I glanced in each and every bar first and then I went to the gym, the casino, and even the gift shop. No Rick! Finally, I went to the pool deck where people were still sitting by the pool and enjoying themselves. No Rick! Then, I happened by the poolside buffet and there he was. Rick was eating a grilled sandwich. It turns out he had discovered that each day it was the place to go where they grill sandwiches any way you wish. He was the regular who appeared every day for the first sandwich of the day!

Because he was so happy with that sandwich, he was also oblivious to me, my worry, or that I stood there watching him. I questioned him, "So this is where you have been every day? I wondered where you have been disappearing to." Rick squinted in the sun and had a big smile on his face for he had found "the place to be" at five o'clock in the evening.

From that day on, those who knew us, called it, "Rick's Place" and the name stuck for the rest of the trip!

Advice When Things Get Messy

Remembering that traveling 24/7 with anyone can have its moments. We all need some space and time. When traveling in a group, designate a meeting place/time so each can go off on their own. There are so many activities and new things to try. You will have lots of stories to tell each other and will meet other cruisers as well.

Often, many travelers get tired, moody, or have jet lag. Hopefully, it won't happen to you, but most have some little disagreement of some kind. That is a lot of minutes, hours, and days, to be together. I will never forget a couple at our dining table celebrating their twenty-fifth wedding anniversary. They were delightful and so happy to be cruising together. I never asked what their argument was about, but she went to the cabin. In her anger, she ironed all of their clothes to keep busy and unwind. Thankfully, they made up, and then … they were the best-dressed couple on the ship. Every outfit they wore was pressed and they looked so wonderful hand-in-hand neatly strolling the decks.

Creamy Mashed Potatoes

At the beginning of a cruise, it seems almost everyone asks each other, "Have you cruised before? How many times?" I guess it is a general conversation, but then there is always the one who says, "I have cruised seven times and ...." Or the one, "Well, I have cruised seventeen times and ...." There should not even be a, shall we call it – "know-it-all," because after all, every cruise is unique and special. I personally stopped counting after 101+ cruises, and I do not say a word. I listen. Whether one is there for their first cruise or however many, we are all boarding the same ship for an adventure. We can't possibly know what it is until we experience it. The ports, the people, the entertainment, music, sounds, and hurrah, are all the qualities that make cruising ever so special.

I was cruising with some friends and John said one day, "If anyone else starts boasting I just don't know what I will do. I will do something though." We didn't think anything of it ... until it happened. You had to be there to understand the event; four people sat at our table for an open seating luncheon. Though they were together, each one-upped the other non-stop. "Let me tell you about my thirtieth cruise and I already know everything there is to know about these ports." "I've tried all of the entrees before, and I can tell you what to order." And, on and on it went on until one of them looked at John, who hadn't had a chance to even say a word, and condescendingly said, "Oh, this must be your very first cruise?"

He did do something. John put his head down … right into the creamy mashed potatoes on his plate! First stunned in astonishment … then everyone began to laugh! How do you explain such "un-cruise" behavior to those around you? Well, we managed to, and all listened. From then on, more people thought about just being who they are and taking in the joys of the cruise experience. It is a first for all, the cruise experience unfolds and the ship sails on.

Taste Trials

Traveling with Michael is a rewarding and different experience as he wants to get out into the world and explore as much as possible. I believe his passport is his prized possession. It represents immigration into countries near and far with some worldly passport stamps that are rare, exotic, and of intrigue. My wanderlust has rubbed off on him. Quality one-on-one time together is amusing, memorable, and an exploration day in and day out. An epic adventure is forever Michael's goal. There are challenges with anyone you travel with and simultaneously we open our eyes and minds to discovery in many directions.

Words Shared by My Son, Michael Whiteman ...

Cruising is a chance to try things you've only maybe heard of yet never seen. The tastes and smells are all enticing. The waiters are friendly and fun as they share their love for food and life. No matter what the culture, it is nice to try food from around the world. Cruisers learn about other interests, flavors, and specialties.

Cruising is the unique opportunity to try

culturally diverse dishes. Escargot. Caviar. Lutefisk. Octopus. Fiskekaker. Poutine. Pufferfish. It might sound and look scary but end up being a delight. Not paying a lot and skeptical to try is a plus because no one is questioning if you decide it is not a taste for you.

I like the multiple courses and the myriad of different options. My most favorite is that I like all that I try. Life in the dining room is one delight, yet so are the buffets, pizzas, and don't forget room service. I feel spoiled in the morning to have oatmeal with many options which I include every time. (Raisins, nuts, fresh blueberries.)

I have shared with my cousins, friends, and others about discovering foods from the far corners of the world. It is fun to introduce them to culinary and savory flavors and aroma. Whether we dine with a new flavor, zest, or tang in our appetizers, it also is apparent in the wines or desserts in accompaniment. The ambiance is enhanced, and the energy of the cruise enriched.

Craving Prawns

I sat at a shared table on formal night. A lovely couple from the UK joined my friend Clare and me. The fellow said he was craving prawns and how could he possibly get them. I said ask for it – usually, the dining room can accommodate cravings and such.

So – he asked the assistant waiter for prawns. The assistant waiter asked the waiter for prawns. The waiter asked the head waiter for prawns. The headwaiter asked the maitre d' for prawns. So much commotion! Passengers have asked for more unusual tastes over the years. It did not seem that outrageous to me.

We continued a nice conversation and waited to see if the wish would come true. Finally, the moment the waiter returned with an unquestionable smile. (The passenger is always right?) A dish was placed in front of the gentleman who quickly looked at me. "Gail, what is this?" In the china dish on formal night was the delicacy. Mission accomplished. Not! In that dish were – Prunes!

So … that is why the assistant waiter had turned to the waiter who consulted the head waiter who approached the maitre d'. They didn't feel it appropriate to ask a guest why he wanted prunes on formal night. Maybe it was the accent or just a misunderstanding. The dining staff thought maybe the man really needed some prunes after all?

I wish I could find that couple again. It was one of those curious moments of non-stop laughter that stopped the entire dining room that evening.

Foodie – or – Not

I don't think I am a "foodie" – Maybe a funny "foodie."

Dave always says my brother, Hal, and I should write a His and Her book. Hal pursued his passion for wonderful food and wine with his membership in and leadership of the Confrérie de la Chaîne des Rôtisseurs. It is the world's oldest, largest, and most prestigious food and wine society. Hal Small held many offices within it, including being its President/Bailli Délégué of the USA chapter. He was honored with membership in the American Academy of Chefs and made a lifetime member in the American Culinary Federation. He has an enormous understanding of wines and good food from throughout the world and has received numerous awards and fulfillment for his extraordinary work. Hal has enjoyed unique dining experiences at restaurants throughout the world, including those that are "bucket list" and Michelin starred. Sister, me, Gail, prefer snacks, out-of-the-way places, roadside/or health food.

Sometimes in travel, it is a quest of what I can and do discover in local foods. It is the essence of cultures and moments and tastes shared. It is said that a culinary experience fills the soul. Authentic food dishes are often a travel discovery. I am petite and do not have a large appetite. A taste of this or that, and a meal here or there, is enough for me, and it (Drives Dave crazy!) Local dishes can be a culinary masterpiece.

For example, a one day in Boston. The highlight for me was when Dave and I wandered the streets and sights. A smell permeated the air and aha – followed it – only to find a food truck. They had hot homemade sourdough crusty bread with melted Brie cheese over thin slices of freshly sliced pear. The blend was unique and flavorful with a taste that was sweet and juicy.

Every place, every country, has its style of cuisine/cooking and that is what makes travel and exploration so intriguing. Recipes, flavors, tastes, and discussions often ignite conversations on the subject of food that can be endless. Dining experiences at all levels offer the opportunity for conversations and learning and, many times, lead to friendships that may become lifelong.

Different Times

When I first started cruising eating was in the traditional dining room or a buffet was available. Alternate choices were not a possibility. The plentiful midnight buffet was a cruise highlight for many. It started with an endless line at 11:30 p.m. for taking pictures and the partaking of food at – midnight. Ice carvings dazzled all amidst theme music and an ambiance like no other. A feast of intricately carved foods and every culinary delight imaginable. Some looked almost too good to eat. People these days though are a little more conscious of what they consume – especially after midnight. Ships next offered chocolate buffets and maybe some still do. Everything chocolate! (Kind of like being a kid in Willy Wonka's Chocolate Factory.) A dessert bar of mousses, pastries, dipped fruits, beverages, and everything/anything possible (beyond imaginable) for the chocolate connoisseur. I did observe some chocolate buffets given around a pool deck where a lot melted – either that on display for eating or dishes left here and there.

A Cruise Ship First

Mom and I sailed on a ship and we enjoyed her favorite, of course, a chocolate fondue. Also, cheese fondue (for me) was available. It was a fun alternative to a lavish meal in the main dining room. A different characteristic and choice in cruising. The relaxed freedom and flexibility of freestyle dining had begun. It was recommended to leave $5 in the middle of the table as a thank you tip. Soon after specialty dining followed among many cruise lines taking specific reservations to savor and indulge in more choices and specialty foods. Today, as we know, there are more eateries, grills, and cafes offering a variety of tastes and experiences.

Tempting Choices

Do you have a favorite food when cruising? Dining

is a "celebration" crafted to please cruisers on a culinary adventure. Multi-course options and meals with enhanced flavors and choices are enticing and plentiful. "Mouthwatering and mesmerizing" can describe unforgettable cruise fare. Allergies? The best strategy is to let the dining room know of special dietary needs so they can accommodate you. Allergies differ and kitchens have policies to avoid cross-contamination while preparing appropriate meals and even some gourmet surprises. What a pair, Dave is gluten-free, and I have an allergy to sulfites, and we have feasted just fine. Know though that there is a significant someone special in that kitchen with the sole responsibility of preparing all of the special meals. We all applaud the waiters and dining staff. If you have any special food needs that are followed oh so carefully, ask, if possible, to meet the exceptional culinary chef to show your appreciation and acknowledgment.

Gastronomic Cruise Ship Discoveries off the Ship

We tucked into the mountains on our excursion on the chilly day the ship cruised into Maine. The sea coast scenery and trails contained picturesque panoramas. We walked a street with quaint harbor shops and eateries. Lobster rolls and chowder were the popular tastes of Portland. Suddenly the thought of something we never ate, was somehow appealing. Hot wild blueberry pie! We ordered one piece to share and found a log on the side of the road. Perfect! As if reserved just for us! We sat down together, and you would think we were at a five-star gourmet spot of fine dining. To us, it truly was – steaming hot pie with incredible crust and ice cream that melted all over. We shared one paper plate, one fork, and one napkin to wipe the mess off our faces. What do they say – Yum, yum good! We haven't had wild blueberry pie before or after that day, yet the memory is one of those travel stories that always stays with us.

Actually, the first food trucks I ever encountered were a discovery when off a ship on an early evening strolling in Papeete. Dozens of colorful popular food trucks were concentrated at Place Vaiete Square and though we say we eat too much on ships, this was enticing. We shared with others from the ship and ordered what seemed like one of everything. It was delicious, especially the island spices and content were different than cruise cuisine. (Recipes I wish I now had – I can almost taste that food even now, today.)

Walking in Greece I could hardly believe my eyes. In a small quaint corner window of a tiny shop was a gal in a cute, blue, and white ruffled uniform holding the largest cookie sheet I had ever seen. She took up the whole window holding Spanakopita, the tasty Greek savory flaky phyllo dough pie filled with spinach, eggs, and feta. Yum. A tradition of ancient Greece that is difficult to make because of the crisp thin layers that tend to fall apart. Greek folk music was playing in that open-air courtyard as I walked in. We spoke none of the same language though she knew – I craved the largest slice possible. Ahh – out I walked for one of the happiest of all meals of my travels. I ate it all too!

And, that night I suffered not because I was still full, but because I was not very popular with the waiters in the dining room. I was so full that I could not imagine ordering nor eating dinner. They tried everything, offering the whole shebang, and all I opted for was a coffee latte.

On a ship, you can try many entrees that you might not have at home. Dave and fellow diners at our table ordered the lamb shanks. I looked the other way – EWW! They of course had no interest in my spinach delicacy and story, and they were happy in their own element. To each their own! Dave has his own favorite too when he discovered congee for breakfast on cruise ships. It is a broth with rice submerged and includes different spices and ingredients. (Often, different each time.)

Shhhh … I would be happy to even skip the main dining room. Sit down dinners with multi-course meals, so much food, and it does take hours. I know for some it is the performance and presentation of the china and silver, the fine dining experience. And, they do say, "don't be bashful have as much as you wish." If traveling with Dave or Michael, it is to the dining room we go. When traveling with Carrie or other girl-friends, we like to discover the variety in the buffet. Especially, the award-winning cakes and pies that can be described as decadent. I took photographs of the assorted pastries that each in itself is like a master-mind art project. The head chef appeared to inquire what exactly I was doing. I clarified that the confection art was astounding and creative, indescribable and I wanted to capture the look of it all. (I did taste the bubbling stuffed baked apples and baked fruit and fresh berries.)

Distinctive Plus Delicious

I know that every reader has their own stories of food favorites, mishaps, and cravings. The memories last and the smell and taste almost do too. I read that a place deep downstairs in a dark German railway station had the best homemade soup. Of course – a quest to find the Bahnhof. I went down steep flights of stairs, I do not speak any German, and I did smell something cooking. I liked the delicacy of tasty hot homemade soup made of chicken broth and noodles with potatoes, garnished with lemon, bay leaves, peppercorns, cloves, and split peas along with an accompanying wedge of homemade rye bread. When ready to walk back up every one of those stairs and return to the ship, I was presented with a piece of apple strudel. One never knows what we can find on a personal excursion in a foreign land.

When a ship pulls into Barcelona the Port Vell terminal is at the southernmost end of the famous Ramblas. There is transportation available, yet it is a nice walk in a trading seaport on the coast of the Mediterranean. The Columbus monument is a sculptured landmark and many still question which way he is pointing. They say Barcelona represents over 2000 years of history that date to the time of the Ancient Romans. My favorite is the medieval streets and diverse archaeological heritage. Barcelona is the place to discover Antoni Gaudi, the famous modernistic architect. Gaudi buildings are unusual and unmistakable. What time is dinner? Typically, after 9 or 10 p.m. and well into the next morning. Barcelona is known for its tapas culture. The Spanish cuisine is served on small plates as an appetizer or snack. Regions of Spain have savory types and tastes of tapas to share though it is about relaxing and sharing the experience.

Paella means "large frying pan" in Catalan and Valencian. It is a mixture of ingredients blended together with rice, oil, and garlic. Paella to Dave and I is our favorite in Barcelona. Walking out of the Mediterranean cruise terminal a balcony overlooks, flowers blossoming, birds fluttering onto the steps, and that is our go-to place. The pan is gigantic and sizzling hot, the tasty ingredients not to be matched yet. Pair Paella with freshly squeezed fruit in Sangria in a glass pitcher and the taste/experience is local and phenomenal. Barcelona is a place with unique style and ambiance, vibrant with art and culture.

Heavy pouring rain, feet, and shoes became mush, sopping wet, yet Michael and I continued to wander the tiny narrow streets in the heart of the old city of Old Town, Genoa. Always a limited time in port when on a cruise ship, so the rain did not stop us. There was a small one-room trattoria, so Michael dashed in to buy an Italian delicacy made by the magic hands of a pizza chef. Fresh rich tomato sauce, creamy cheese, basil, and extra virgin olive oil plus fresh toppings of mushrooms and spices. Italian pizza sculptured like a piece of thick cake deep-dish style. "When the moon hits your eye, like a big pizza pie, That's Amore." In Italy do as the Italians do!

Now writing this, maybe I am a "foodie" of some sort. Or maybe a connoisseur of adventure!

Dave and I reserved a private tour, *Simply Amalfi*, on the Italian coast. We connected online prior to sailing to Italy, found the English good, and Katharine originally from my rival high school in Los Angeles of all things. "See the Amalfi Coast from a local's perspective and drink in the history, culture, and beauty that this land and its people have to offer." We drove high around curves of the jagged steep coast to hills and surrounding coastal areas. Salvatore serenaded us with Italian song and took us to scenic overlooks that gave us extraordinary views of the coastline. We stopped in a small local village where cheese is made daily. The rounds of cheese were images to remember and the scent enticing. The cheesemaker spoke passionately in Italian, and the taste melted in your mouth. We were treated like family and unexpectedly arrived at the home of Katherine and Salvatore overlooking the dramatic Mediterranean landscape. We toasted with homemade wines and a sampling of crunchy, garlicky Italian small bites. Observing the blue sea with spectacular views, homemade pasta was served in authentic ceramic pottery. The experience captured more than words can describe. A "tour" became an unforgettable meal of a lifetime!

Bon Appetit!

What traditions are created in kitchens big or small, here, or there? A "foodie" relishes food for pleasure and the hobby I think is the experiences. Maybe I do qualify as a "foodie." Everyone eats food! And, almost every reader could perhaps write about what texture or taste pleases your palate and senses. My interest is in exploring a wide variety of food experiences and discoveries from all around the globe.

Am I making you hungry? Foods of the world are uniquely traditional while also as fascinating as the people and places.

Lifted Together

One afternoon passengers were engaged in a multitude of activities throughout a ship. The loud announcement interrupting the flow of the day came from the bridge, "All passengers are to stay inside and away from top decks." Those words aroused some suspicion and the next voice over the speaker explained why. "One of our fellow passengers has a health emergency and a helicopter is on its way to hover over the top of the ship so that a basket can be airlifted into the helicopter. For safety, we ask only for deck clearance and passenger cooperation. A medical airlift is underway." It made everyone stop – and think. How sad that someone's cruise vacation was ending with an emergency evacuation at sea. How fortunate that the medical staff had optimism that this medevac airlift would be successful; that the ailing patient was thought to be well enough to endure such a rescue.

Knowing that the family could not fit into the helicopter and must remain onboard was frightening. A bonding took place among strangers, each hoping the best for the rescue and passenger. I thought about it all night, especially thinking about the unknown for the family who could not accompany their loved one so ill. We did receive word the next day that the sick passenger was admitted to a local hospital. And, arrival was just in time to successfully undergo emergency medical treatment in Puerto Rico.

We felt elated that the story was taking on a happy ending. The family was able to disembark at the next port. The tone of the passengers on the cruise changed. Happy for those personally involved, and more aware that life is to appreciate and live fully, each and every day.

Endless Possibilities

Creative writing is the theme for some of my lectures on cruises. Each day is an activity to encourage and stimulate writing! I bring unusual items that nurture cruisers to think, reflect, sometimes laugh out loud and … write. One Australian man seemed to attend most of my talks always with curiosity and a spark. It was I who became curious; who he was, was he traveling alone, writing a journal or book and … whatever? I liked his questions and involvement as well as his Aussie accent.

The Australian man is named Brian. What a surprise when I met his wife, Helen, on the last day exclaiming, "One of my best vacations ever." Really? Brian was happy and engaged in an activity that he shared with her each day. She was content to read and relax with the ocean view and breeze.

I was staying in Australia for one night after the cruise before my long flight home to Los Angeles. "Can we treat you to dinner?" How sweet the thought that they would want to do something for me. And they sure did! Brian picked me up at my hotel and drove me to their house. Always fascinated with the driver on the other side of the car, and looking at the scenery of another continent.

When we reached their home, they were so inviting as hosts and I had to recall, they just disembarked after two weeks of sailing. So, in the corner of the room was quite a sight, suitcases with the contents tumbling out every which way as they had no time to unpack.

Australian wine and some of their favored local dishes were prepared. How they even had time to get to a market and cook seemed miraculous. Fresh fish and a baked pumpkin that was roasted and still the taste is remembered. (In fact, an unexpected surprise arrived in my mail sometime later, pumpkin seeds, which are special as the pumpkins in the states are not similar.)

What a finale to a cruise! Amazing cruisers with such a flair for travel and a warm genuine caring for others.

Sometimes cruising is only the beginning, of long-lasting memories and friendships. Years later, Dave was traveling with me to Australia. So, I wrote to tell Brian and Helen and they insisted we not only see them but to stay with them. And ... we did! Brian took us to a sanctuary with magnificent scenery and a chance for Dave's first up close and personal meeting with kangaroos. A kangaroo leaped forward several feet, eyed Dave who fed it some leaves right out of his hands. We thought that was the highlight of our sharing moments with our Australian friends. Not!

We had the chance to meet and visit with family members of Brian and Helen. We all sat together at a relaxing small-town cafe patio and shared Australian wine and … an order of the pumpkin I had loved. As we reached their new home, different than the one where I previously was spoiled with dinner, surfer Dave could not believe the ocean view! For mere steps from the home, the scenic view of the Australian coast was like that of a travel brochure. A pristine stretch of sand and sea. Sadly, we were leaving early the next morning to catch our flight home to the USA. The next thing we knew though, hospitality unimaginable, we learned that their son was to arrive at 5 a.m. with surfboards for Dave to experience the spectacular stretch of the Aussie Ocean.

Brian and Helen came through the states on their way to a cruise some years later. We had the pleasure of meeting them at LAX airport for some shared moments before they sailed off.

Brian (remember, the participant of my creative writing lectures) contributed a story of his clown experiences in my *Joyful Volunteering* book. Brian told me the story of someone surprising him with custom clown shoes as his were make-do from plastic bags of sort. "If that is volunteering, it is just the most beautiful thing!" Brian Ramsey.

Celebrations! Memories! The little things that intrigue and keep one traveling. The planning and destination of a voyage often are not the most significant, for it can be the unexpected, the discoveries of travel that make it all come alive.

Seeing the Seam

Twas the first ship built in 1970 for one particular cruise line. Beautiful. Powerful. Remarkable. Surprisingly comfortable. Seafaring: To travel the world's oceans. And then ... returned? How do they return an entire cruise ship? It was sent back to the Finnish shipyard to create a midsection that could be added into the middle of her hull. And then, putting her pieces all back together again?!

S-t-r-e-t-c-h and 1 + 1 + 1 + 1 = One master, one staff captain, one chief engineer and one cruise director!

They said it accomplished improved profits and included forty percent more capacity. (If only there was an easy reverse procedure for passengers who say they put on too many pounds in their midsection?)

Anyway, I was curious and eager to return on this very same ship as soon as it was enlarged and reintroduced. A maddening experience because it was so seamless and aligned that I could not find any evidence. I got a lot of extra exercise! (Maybe I appeared to be a spy as I meandered up and down the long corridors on each and every level and found nothing.)

An Eternal Night in the Eternal City

Shared by Friend and Editor Cindy Mihaly ...

We were on our way to Rome, the port of call for our cruise around the Mediterranean. After researching our voyage for over a year the time had finally come.

After a layover in London, we were informed on our connecting flight that because of a catering strike, we would only be served light snacks and drinks. Regretting not eating dinner at the airport in London, we figured it was no problem; we'll eat in Rome. And, we could almost already taste the scrumptious food awaiting us on the ship! Our cruise of a lifetime was on final approach.

After 15 hours of flying and layovers, we thankfully landed in Rome, the departure destination on our cruise itinerary. Upon arriving in the evening, tired and hungry, we went to retrieve our luggage and when it did not appear, panic started to set in. Even though I had made sure to pack a little of everything in each bag in case a situation like this arose, the only bag that made the flight was the one that housed our formal wear for the cruise!

While filling out forms to retrieve our lost luggage, my husband was getting a lesson on how not to convert our money into Euros at an ATM. His first attempt failed because of a broken machine but soon after he found another machine, this time with success.

We were then off to meet our driver who was to take us to our hotel for that night. Little did we know when I arranged for a driver ahead of time that he would only speak ... Italian? In no time he was leading us on a long adventure; apparently, our hotel was one of the hardest to find in the entire city!

As the car we were in cruised through Rome, the driver stopped several times to ask for directions from a number of the locals, all more than willing to help and each with their own idea of the location of the hotel. We watched with amusement as they conversed, speaking with hand gestures into the air as much as words. He eventually came down the street the wrong way and managed to lead us into a parking lot which with each turn got narrower and narrower until we barely squeezed through. He then convinced oncoming traffic to back out of the roadway so he could get through. It was so comical I told my husband, "I hope you're getting this on video?"

When we weren't going around in circles, going down one-way streets the wrong way, we were fascinated by our glimpses of the remains of ancient Rome. Seeing the Colosseum spectacularly lit up for the night, we sat there in awe as it was a sight to behold.

With the help of the locals, our driver finally found our hotel, actually the hotel across the street from our hotel. He dropped us off with the only luggage we had, and I think he was a bit surprised to see us walk across the street to the opposite hotel. It was approaching midnight; we checked in and were given directions to a little café down the street. They were closed yet gracious enough to serve us a light snack.

We sat and reminisced about the entire evening. We truly had a night to remember. Seeing the sights, sounds, and people throughout the adventures of a cruise experience certainly puts things into perspective.

Our lost luggage arrived later the next day, and our day had finally come to board the ship. Our driver did not hesitate to get us to the ship; he drove more like Mario Andretti and got us there in record time!

We were amazed at our first glimpse of the ship – she was just beautiful and huge, the largest ship to set sail in the Mediterranean and brand new. When we boarded and set sail we were in heaven and were looking forward to all the wonderful and exciting things we were going to see and do. Twelve days of relaxation, food, sightseeing, entertainment and did I say food? Our waiters every night were a delight and especially when they serenaded me on my birthday.

We took time for relaxation and that included room service. We would look forward to sitting on our balcony in the mornings sipping coffee while coming into the different ports. We looked out to see turquoise waters and experienced the ambiance of cruising.

There were so many highlights during our cruise, but none better than seeing the tiny island of Stromboli spewing lava into the evening sky from our ship and sailing into Venice, such a heartfelt experience. What better way to see and do all that we did? What started as a night of blunders ended as an adventure of a lifetime and I hope to one day be able to experience it again.

After all – I did throw that coin into the Trevi Fountain!

If He Only Knew

I cruised with my son Michael who was maybe 18 at the time. We have an understanding when we travel together, that is to swim and relax and play during the day, however, dinner is always together. The waiters enjoy Michael sitting at their table since he genuinely enjoys food and tries every kind of texture and taste. When they tempt him with seconds or an unusual dish, he usually does not decline. Don't we all wish we could feast like that and not gain an ounce? On one particular cruise, we were seated at the captain's table. A friendly Greek captain who spoke little to no English yet somehow, we all communicated. As soon as the appetizers, soups, salad, and main course were complete, Michael politely excused himself with a warm smile. That was our agreement and that was fine, for we dined together.

One of the staff on that cruise was someone I had encountered on another ship. He was an officer originally from Jamaica, a place that I love. We had shared stories about the Jamaican Irie spirit. Every time I returned to our cabin a surprise awaited, always with a friendly note and a different delight. One time it was chocolate-covered strawberries, another it was canapés, fruits, tea-sized sandwiches with different fillings, and even beautiful long stem red roses. I guess you would call it "re-gifting" because that is what I did. I told Michael to share the goodies with his new-found friends. He was a popular young cruiser and made quite an impression.

To Be or Not To Be

Careful where you sit in the audience? Most of us do not want to be the person singled out in the crowd by the comedian entertainer.

The show started and out of a full audience Dave was "it." It is difficult to refuse the call to the stage as it will call more attention to you. So, up he went on the stage and another fellow was also summoned to join in.

First, they were asked to do a very simple dance step. That went OK even though it was a bit stiff and awkward. Next, they were asked to do a seemingly easy chorus of a song. This in terms of pitch, timing, and correct recitation of lyrics were far more of a struggle.

Finally, came the culmination. This newly formed duo was asked to do the ultimate by both singing and dancing at the same time. Oh my. Modeled and prodded by the comedian, this was their chance to shine in the spotlight. Not! (They proved not to be the next Fred Astaire nor Gene Kelly.)

Cries of laughter in the audience erupted. The saving grace was the other man called up was a worse dancer than Dave. It seemed to me like forever he was up there until finally, it was over. He returned to his seat with the roar of applause.

The very next comedy show two nights later we were safely sitting midship nowhere to be noticed. (We thought!) Audience members slouched in their chairs and looked this way and that. Our plan of anonymity utterly had failed. Out of the capacity crowd, the comedian picked me to speak directly to the audience to entertain with dialogue as part of the show. Uh oh.

The most difficult question was fired at me for everyone to hear, "What is your name?" I was laughing so hard I could not say my name. Of course, that fed the comedian and so on it went. And then, she noticed Dave sitting next to me, and that was enough to enhance her show. "You are with ... him?!" Tension and energy in the room built as a constant stream of laughs ensued.

Going "Home"

I was cruising on the latest built mega-ship and as the ship pulled into the port of Nagasaki the blaring blast of the horn rang out. The local crowd went wild. People were everywhere bursting with screams and song. Musical groups were parading and playing, pom-poms and flags were waving, and massive colorful banners were displayed on walls all along the pier.

This was the first time this ship sailed into Nagasaki since the day construction was complete and it embarked on its maiden voyage. The ship was built there. The town people and officials lined the streets and came out to welcome home the ship. The scene was like one might see in a movie, but we were experiencing it. The Chief engineer on the ship had actually liveds in Japan when the ship was being built. The celebration was unique for him and his wife as they returned. It was fun to be on the open deck standing at the railing with maybe 2000 cruisers on our ship. The feeling was what cruising is all about, the jubilant moments and the camaraderie.

As we snapped pictures and moved to the music, the finale was when the fireboats surrounded the ship and welcomed us. A magnificent water salute was performed honoring the ship. The water they squirted resembled spectacular multicolored waterfalls. The sun shining through the sprays of water became that of a beautiful rainbow.

Captain Knows Best

Ahh, the pink sands on the British island of Bermuda with a distinctive blend of cultures. The town crier and the ringing of a bell – such a welcome greeting. Bermuda shorts are the norm one can't help but notice in the charming town. Bermudians wear them for business attire and even cocktail parties – to be worn three inches above the knee. A relaxing escape in cove-type beaches is a possibility as are the panorama views. Scattered through the island are historic forts, the dockyard, museums, parks, and caves. The rum swizzle is the cocktail named after Bermuda's oldest pub, the Swizzle Inn, featuring a comfortable friendly atmosphere. (FYI – my souvenir hat says – "Swazzle Out.")

We walked a pathway to a cove noting crystal clear waters, steep cliffs, and pristine sand. Dave was in the water in no time, and I relaxed quietly observing the stunning view while sipping my diet coke. My quiet serene moments were interrupted by a lady who talked non-stop. She was from a different ship and laughed so when I finally said we had to go. At times, winds prevail as Bermuda's ocean winds are tempered by the Gulf Stream. I explained that when our captain spoke, he said we must cruise early because of impending weather conditions and winds that have been known to be tricky.

One always wonders when in the waters approaching Bermuda. The "Bermuda Triangle?" Who knows the whole truth, yet ships are thought to have disappeared under mysterious circumstances. All but a mystery? There is a very real "Bermuda Triangle" some readers might even be a victim of? It is the Disneyland "Bermuda Triangle" called that because they say 200+ sunglasses mysteriously appear each and every day in the Magic Kingdom parks. I read that over the years it is estimated that 1.65 million pairs of sunglasses have been lost there.

Dave reluctantly got out of the alluring waters, and we walked the path back to the ship. My favorite place to be when leaving a port is in a hot tub on top. So, there we were soaking in a Jacuzzi when we witnessed the "other" ship sailing out before us! (Aha – the ship of that lady on the beach who had laughed at me.) Unfortunately, her ship sailed on without her.

Thank You, Captain!

I should share that on a previous Bermuda cruise the ship also left early, in a big hurry. Crew alerted passengers out on excursions and beaches to return to the ship. The ship sailed without the golfers. (They returned to the ship that was not even there = the pier was empty.) Staff was there to escort a return to the ship and … quite a story to tell.

Oh, the hassle of moving through Cuba immigration, one at a time, presenting the visas and documents that were almost impossible to obtain. Once over the border, the anticipation, fear, and fascination of Cuba took over. We changed our money into the then-required CUC and Cuban Peso. Our awaiting Blexie guide was bubbly with commentary and answers to questions while sharing knowledge about Cuban sites, history, and customs. Cuba is long known for its American cars lining its streets. Part of the thrill was the classic car that was ours for the day with the proud driver that completed this fascinating duo. Our well-preserved '55 Chevy was buffed to a shine with colors of brilliant bright ruby red and vivid white. Classic cars are vital to the Cuban culture. The vintage restored cars are modified and held together with odd parts and scrap metal. A day truly of stepping back in time. (Oh – I could see the look in Dave's eyes – that wish to ship a car home as his – souvenir.)

Most of Havana was built before the 1960s and buildings have not seen much upkeep since. Snap! I stopped in a plaza with cold war relics to take a picture of the boulevard and buildings. A little lady with a cigar in her mouth appeared out of nowhere with her hand out and oh, that expression on her face. We didn't have small bills so her CCU's tip was more than ample.

A Full Day with Knowing – We Have to Go Back!

The captain made an announcement before leaving the ship that we would have to return by 1 a.m. This was worrisome because Cuba's famous El Tropicana Night Club spectacular was the splurge we had reserved for the evening. We were looking forward to the cabaret and Cuban food, costumes, rhythm, song, and dance.

I remembered the captain speaking to change the ship departure hour not once, but three times. Sadly hot, tired, and disappointed, we had to forego the rest of our Cuban adventure and walked towards the ship. I once heard people say that a memorable moment of cruising is when chilled washcloths are handed to them upon returning to a ship on a hot day. Yes, this was a sizzling hot day, large towels were not chilled, they were pool towels thrown to us as we cleared customs and neared the ship security check-in. Just in time! The predicted storm was already upon us, torrential rain and towels were an attempt to cover us though we got drenched from head to toe. Appreciative of the crew that struggled to keep us dry and hopefully all were onboard as per the captain's instructions as we sailed off amidst noisy rumbling thunder.

Dave and I were excited to be scheduled to return in a cruise circumnavigation of Cuba. I cried the day the news proclaimed that Americans are no longer permitted to travel to Cuba by ship due to U.S. government policy changes. (2019 on my birthday – I remember the day.) It will happen in the future, I just hope.

◆ ◆ ◆

5 a.m. security check as Dave and I entered the bridge. We were in Alaskan waters. The captain and crew were attentive managing the vessel and all that this entails. The bridge is off-limits to passengers on most ships because of the critical nature of operations there. The windows are extensive, binoculars are in use by those on watch, and officers in the cockpit area guide the vessel. The bridge is where the captain and trained seamen control and command the ship.

Dave as a cartographer and naturalist was to give the narration on loudspeakers to passengers out on the deck and throughout the ship to understand and observe glaciers. On this particular early day, the captain in his presiding chair with binoculars in hand conveyed that the entry to a bay and glacier views were questionable. It was a wait-and-see. Entering waterways depended on timing, icebergs, weather elements, and the overall welfare of the ship, crew, and passengers.

We waited. Snow-capped mountains and a hanging glacier faced us. Migratory birds were in the air. A glacier-carved landscape is something one has to witness to believe. Giant glacier ice calving is a sight to see and hear as glaciers appear above and below the water and put on an unbelievable show of nature. The captain wanted us to have this experience.

And, we waited ... Yet because of real-life obstacles we did not quite make our destination. Massive icebergs and fog banks blocked our path. We were at what was like a watery fork in the road. We were at the mouth of two diverging fjords and experienced this pristine place. What we saw was a hanging glacier close to the locale of an abandoned mining location and tribal village. It was clear, crisp, and beautiful. Plus, the captain gave us a gift of safety.

While waiting and waiting, it was me speaking to the captain and crew, "I wish a whale would jump up … right now." Like a fairytale … or make-believe movie, at that extraordinary minute, facing me, in front of the bridge and an entire cruise ship breached … A whale!

Matching Pairs

Once when I was checking in to board a ship there was a special enthusiasm of passengers in the air. I observed smiles, anticipation, and the typical semi-confusion until all are welcomed and comfortable once onboard. I spotted a nicely dressed young woman quietly enter the area hand-in-hand with her partner and watched as she began to softly mumble something ... and then out loud. Suddenly she started screaming, "Oh, oh, what have you done?" Everyone ... stopped to watch. Her face was red, tears started streaming down her face, and I thought I saw just a hint of a smile. Waiting passengers' eyebrows raised, shoulders shrugged, and ... she in some way disappeared into the crowd.

That night in the dining room I was escorted to my assigned table for the cruise and to my surprise, coincidentally, this same couple was seated at my table. So, I got the whole scoop. Her husband had promised her a little time together with a reservation for a romantic lunch by the water in San Pedro. She thought she was being led into a restaurant when she noticed a line. She witnessed a crowd and people holding carry-on luggage, so she was completely bewildered. (What he had done was – planned a romantic cruise, not giving her as much as a clue.) A friend dropped their suitcases curbside with their luggage tags and cabin number. Friends and family had everything covered for their two children, the house, pets, and her work. How fun! Everyone knew, but her, the boss, the children's teachers, and the neighbors.

As you can imagine, sitting at that table was full of excitement and energy. It was their first cruise. She couldn't believe it. And remember, he had packed for her too! She had more than enough outfits to choose from throughout the cruise. The funny part was that she is one of those people that always has to have shoes to match. So, her husband had packed one entire suitcase of only shoes wanting to be sure he brought the right ones.

"Pennies from Heaven?"

Michael was a typical 13-year-old enjoying a huge cruise ship thanks to his grandma. (My mom.) It was a brand-new modern ship with lots to wander and explore. I will never forget the moment the power of an entire ship abruptly went out. Seriously! Smoke filled the air and obviously, all movement ceased. (A little/lot of uncertainty.) In days past many cruisers smoked so the smoke and smell filled the air almost instantaneously. Michael's worst fear was that grandma might be stuck in an elevator. He rushed to find her and thankfully she was not. It seemed like forever, yet everything finally resumed to normal.

The three of us enjoyed the lure of cruising. Special times together to always remember. Ready for action Michael found his way to the casino and security never bothered to shoo him out. His game of chance was lucky. He hit jackpots of quarters, buckets of them actually, and was one fortunate 13-year-old. Coins accumulated over a weeks' time, and he stashed a bucketful in the corner of his narrow top bunk.

That was the night in our cabin that I decided to have Mom help me to take out my cornrow braids from our visit to Jamaica. (54 of them.) She was not too pleased as that is a tedious exhausting endeavor. The styled geometric lines adorned with beads were stylish while they lasted, yet I decided it was time. The intricate final braid was finally undone, and exhaustion hit so to sleep we went. Until – in the middle of the night – something began to tumble down from Michael's top bunk. A thunderous startling bang with a ringing noise as clanging coins flew here, there, and everywhere.

Pennies from heaven? Not! Just an abundance of treasured coins Michael collected and stored safely on his top bunk.

I think the song/movie with that phrase is an expression about the unexpected. This "rain" was far from expected and a memory we can only laugh at now.

So Lost and Far from Home

Have you ever been told to take contact information of where you are staying or going, or better still, a business card if they have one? This is something important to remember.

I arrived in Russia for a voyage to sail to places I had not previously been. All were welcomed upon our arrival by a young woman in a colorful costume and a charming welcoming smile. She held the round bread and we each broke off a piece which was a symbol to welcome one and all, coming together, in their land. We had hours until sailing and that meant time to explore – Russia.

Walking down the staircase in the subway I noticed what was like a work of art. Murals of color and splendor were everywhere. Art deco wall panels, marble floors, and ceilings of distinctive mosaics. (It's worth a journey to see the uniqueness of it all.) The Moscow subway is famous for its extravagant and unique interior design. Revered as the "Palace of the People."

I got on the subway and smiled at Russians who seemed curious about who I was and where I was going. I took the subway through villages in Moscow. It was a fascinating beginning to a journey so far away from home. I stood in the middle of the remarkable Red Square not knowing where to look first and felt the history. I couldn't believe that I was really there. If only some of those walls and towers could talk. So much to know and learn, and I was right there beginning to experience a land I had not yet traveled.

I returned to the subway and next, I got off and looked all-around at the village. I found everything to be fascinating. There were fresh fragrant flowers, the scent of baked bread, and I observed locals wearing a variety of aprons and outfits.

After a brisk walk, I decided it was time to return to the ship. After my next ride on the subway, things seemed confusing. Though I got off where I thought I was supposed to, nothing looked familiar. Nothing. It had never occurred to me that languages could be so very different. The language of Russia was nothing like English nor any words I have acquired in other travels and countries. I was speechless. Of course, next, I pulled out the card with the name and address of the ship knowing that was the thing to do. This was of no help. It had never occurred to me that there are people who cannot read. (This can happen in every country/anywhere, I since have been told.) The card was in Russian, the language of the land, and no one I asked could understand the words printed on the card.

Lost – in Russia! Of all places, and all times, when a ship was about to sail. My ship! I got back on the subway, scrambling, and went one more stop thinking something had to help. Sure enough, I had gotten off one stop too soon. I retraced my steps walking faster with every step and reached the gangway. Imagine that I, world traveler Gail, could be lost in Russia. Yes, I sure was!

Saving at Sea

On a world cruise en route to Curacao we were having a nice time and strolled into the theater for the evening production. Suddenly we could feel a sway as the ship came to an abrupt stop. Unexpected. Scary. The loudspeaker went on throughout the entire ship. The captain explained that we had indeed halted at the order of Marine Rescue and were immediately turning around to answer distress calls from a stricken vessel. "We must sail 60 nautical miles to reach stranded men in a boat at sea." That was the frightening news, not that our cruise was being changed, but that people were in danger in the middle of the vast ocean.

Showtime somehow continued with elaborate music and dance though most of our focus was on hope and prayers for others in prevailing conditions. As the curtain closed the speaker came on once more. The announcement was ... "the boat sank." It was pitch dark out, waters swelled, and what sea creatures lurked the cold-deep, rough seas. This all took our breath away. And then, word came that a number of men were forced to take to their life raft. Ohhhhhh. Welcome news – it came – "they were all still alive!"

Our cruise ship lowered a rescue boat with hopes of reaching those stranded at sea. To the rescue! Sailors in peril. It was the middle of the night, and we did not go out to watch. We thought to stay out of the way not knowing what we would witness. It took until just before midnight when our brave skilled rescue team successfully saved three men from their raft in the Southern Caribbean Sea. Far from everything they somehow had survived the dangers.

Every once in a while, the story resurfaces in the news with accolades and pictures of the heroic rescue team and the men whose lives they saved.

This Is the Captain Speaking ...

It is said that the success of a ship's voyage lies on the captain's shoulders. The Master of the Ship has wide-ranging expertise. I think of a captain to be adventurous, confident, conscientious, genuine, and dedicated. Day-to-day or weeks and months, navigating harbors and waterways and seaworthiness. I often marvel at the nautical responsibility. Just pulling into port, or backing into port, and sometimes the intriguing 360° maneuver to view ancient glaciers or brilliant flowing volcanoes.

While writing articles and with books in the works, I relished in the rare opportunity to spend time with the captain of a ship. **Captain Attilio Guerrini was born in Tuscany, Italy. He first went to sea at the age of fourteen. He has been in command of many ships and itineraries. When not sailing, home is either in Tuscany or Queensland's Gold Coast of Australia. His family includes his wife Joanne and their daughters, Annalisa and Francesa.**

I visited Captain Guerrini on the Bridge where we shared cappuccinos and toasted to the sea and seeing the world. We talked about his many voyages and experiences:

My career started with fishing and being on a fishing boat. I went to the Nautical Institute in Livorno and then I was in the Italian Navy for two years. Next, I was on a cargo ship and traveled on various vessels. In 1990 I joined a passenger ship and that is where I have been ever since.

Traveling is a good experience, and you get to know many places. Cruising is a true sample. One can discover new things, new people, and know of the culture of others. To cruise is to enjoy! This is a way for communication with people of other lands and languages.

It is exciting every time the ship arrives at a port. I like the dragon in Asia which has the meaning of welcome. Experiencing different greetings, we receive fun, excitement and, emotions. When I have the time, I want to go as a tourist and sample places that I have sailed. I want to see more of China and Vietnam and many places to experience the life of the people. Everywhere we go, we always find something new and positive.

Venice is a highlight for me. Ahhh ... The sights and sounds of pulling into Venice.

Captain Guerrini's face lit up sharing about Venice and stories of the sea. I asked him about the vast responsibility of being the captain of a ship. He responded with such a knowing smile saying:

Passengers can unpack once and see the world. You can wake up on a new day and off you go to new ports, new places, as you discover the world.

As for me being the captain of the vessel? You see – it is the crew and creating an organization that works. A crew is collective and truly one unit. Everyone works at different tasks, and it is the entire crew that makes the ship.

We need soul. What is a ship without soul? We all help each other. There's a unique friendship upon the sea. It is the friendship and friends for life that one never forgets.

A ship is a soul.

When I give pirate talks, audiences learn of the misconception and old superstitions that having a woman on board was bad luck. Not! Ships come in all shapes and sizes and so do the passengers, women too! A study would undoubtedly show endless reasons women passengers engage in the leisurely days of cruising. A captain's life is a life at sea. They do though have a "home away from home," often far and wide across the world. Families do not sail with them all the time; they come on occasionally. It seems exciting to have the captain's wife onboard. More so, is seeing a captain's children comfy onboard and glad to be at sea.

That day with the captain his family was onboard sailing and he shared with me:

The kids center is where children like to go. It is special because it is divided by age groups. Enthusiasm of the staff can be contagious. My girls like to go where they can join fun activities and meet others.

Annalisa – The captain's daughter – then age 10:

I like visiting lots of different places and cruising is a way for me to do this. Walking around the ship there is always a lot to see and that is what I really like. I think it is all very interesting. When I am on ships, I go to the children's center which is a fun way for me to meet new friends from other countries. I can speak different languages; English, Italian, and Japanese.

Francesa – The captain's daughter – then age 5:
With a giggle and an adorable smile, she shyly just said:

I really like it here on the ship. I like time with my daddy.

Not Just in the Movies

Mom and I tried to choose the best shore excursions so we could experience the most out of every port. A land-based trip sightseeing is an easy way to explore culture and onshore activities. We picked what we thought to be exciting and enriching as we selected from an array of opportunities. The highlight of one excursion in Spain was the diverse array of specialty nuts, olives, fruits, and grapes. We were greeted by the farmer and family allowing us to leisurely explore their scenic farm and atmosphere. Tasting was a plus and I focused on the award-winning olives and cheeses. The view overlooked vast land that seemed similar I thought to areas of California. Time was limited because of you know, the old have to get back to the ship on time. Only that was not the reason. As welcome as we were made to feel, the reason we were ushered out in such a hurry – was to make room for the bride about to walk down the long scenic aisle.

Tastes were savory, the views stunning, and the ride home was narrated by our guide as we gazed out the windows. We even had a short stop to wander in a local charming village. A young woman traveling by herself befriended Mom and me as we toured, tasted, and explored throughout the day. She was warm and friendly and so interesting. She clearly indicated that she could NOT miss the ship. It was fun sharing some stories and laughs while fully knowing we did have to get back to that ship on time.

Stopping at a charming local cafe in town sharing traditional rice pudding and conversation was an ideal way to end a fantastic day. (That rice pudding though truly is not for me.) We found out why our new travel mate was all by herself. For we discovered that our new friend – was the captain's wife!

Now, the story. Some time ago three young gals graduated college in Canada and their parents surprised them with a graduation gift – a dream trip on a cruise ship. They had, of course, the time of their lives enjoying a once-in-a-lifetime holiday. When they came home one of the girls emphatically told her family that she had truly fallen in love with the captain of the ship. Her parents listened and shattered her dream breaking the news to her that countless cruisers fall in love with the captain – just like in the movies. To make a long story short, she not only fell in love with the captain, but he also fell in love with her. Soon they got married. The parents were thrilled with their daughter's happiness yet a little sad because she would live far from home.

Story to tell. Yes, the captain's wife, my mom, and I spent some other times adventuring together as she was alone during the long days. It must have been meant to be as we shared companionship and our exuberance for travel. Fairy tales I guess can come true.

She longed for her dream to come true – and married her captain!

Creative Glamour

In the middle of a perfect cruise and you know how sometimes some cruisers bring out a little negativity. No way! Grumbling was taking place as the Academy Awards were that very night. People complaining, "They won't do anything, and we need to see such a special occasion." First, it is a different time zone and second, they knew when boarding the ship that the Academy Awards were taking place. Surprisingly though, passengers did receive invitations to an unnamed event in the lounge that required elegant attire.

Our cruise director offered such style, pizzazz, and class! On Oscar night she strolled so statuesquely all throughout the ship in formal gala attire. However, she wasn't only stylish, she was an elegant problem solver.

We walked in the lounge adorned with sparkle and shine, golden balloons, and to our surprise even a life-size replica of the statuette Oscar. The elegantly dressed cruise staff welcomed each and every passenger making them feel prominent as if they had been truly nominated for an academy award. How special to become part of a pretend internationally acclaimed ceremony.

A world-renowned tradition, a symbolic custom, and the actual nominees were named to us in a list. So, we would cast our vote of the nominees in every category. The person predicting the most winners won a bottle of champagne. Runners-up received the most famous prize on a cruise ship – of course, a keychain.

Fun! Unexpected! The improbable Academy Awards night not only took place, but it was also so perfectly planned and done. The feel-good ambiance – indescribable. Throughout the eventful gala evening, photographers snapped photos of passengers standing by the Oscar statuette. The band played music featuring scores from the Best Original Song nominees.

Ceremony! And the envelope, please …

On sea and far from Hollywood, California, the "best" of the lot was portrayed. Large screens throughout the lounge displayed the actual live ceremony with all its glam and excitement. Best picture and accolades are a component of the Academy Awards. Truly crowd-pleasing. Passengers were thrilled as they bonded sharing an unexpected cruise highlight and, we were there well into the late-night early morning.

The nature of shared connections creates a link between passengers, one of the joys of cruising. Though that night, because of time differences, we heard no acceptance speeches. Although, I do remember one that says it all:

"This is such an honor. But the thing that counts the most with me is the friendships, and the love, and the sheer joy we have shared making movies together."— *Meryl Streep, Best Actress, The Iron Lady.*

Since 1929, the most recognized trophy in the world, The Oscar, has stood on the mantels of the greatest filmmakers. And for us, the winner is ... Best unexpected experience on a cruise ship goes to this cruise director and staff for a glamorous night to remember.

Excerpt from My Joyful Parenting Book

My friend Virginia often heard me babble about ships and cruises. I am fascinated with seeing and discovering this vast world, and my parents met on a cruise when they were very young, so "it" is in my blood. Virginia sailed on a cruise to Mexico and she quickly discovered that cruising is not for her! (Meanwhile, at home, I envisioned throughout that entire weekend the "cruise of a lifetime" that I assumed she must have been encountering.) Her young son, Jason, was alone, wandering a ship looking for "something to do" because Mom was in their cabin seasick, very seasick. Upon her return, her tales of voyaging were far different than mine.

Now, I knew Jason well because he was a close friend of my son, and I had often witnessed his sheer creativity and genius. He was always up to something! Especially at Halloween, he had perfected infinite ways to provide ghostly "things" and hanging "surprises" from my front porch as trick-or-treaters arrived. When the Cub Scouts had their first outside all-night sleepover, I magically appeared and shocked the "brave" boys just before the sun was coming up. I had on a full gorilla outfit, and though I was not quite tall enough to comfortably fit inside it, I wore my high heels underneath the realistic-looking gorilla costume. They earned a badge for bravery and camping, and my novel "parent participation" is long remembered by all through ongoing stories. My "magic" was just fun, but Jason's magic today is phenomenal.

It did turn out that Jason's mother absolutely hated cruising, but there is more to be told of what was discovered on that ocean voyage. The journey wasn't a total disaster because opportunities somehow happen. You never know!

Jason Latimer, World Champion of Magic, Tells the Story in His Own Words:

I was about nine years old and I was traveling with my family on a cruise down to Mexico. I was actually running around the deck playing tag with some newfound friends when, through some strange bit of luck, while being chased I literally ran into a performer who worked on the cruise ship. In fact, he was a juggler and the funny thing is that they were looking for a child to use as a "plant" volunteer in the shows during this cruise. Well ... after asking my parents, of course, I agreed and went to rehearsal to learn my lines and to see where and when I was supposed to do what. However, the following act was actually a professional magician. Now up till then, I had never experienced live magic and when the magician took the stage, I sat in awe watching every move. Over and over, I watched him rehearse even when I had no apparent reason to be in the theater. I desperately asked him to teach me something, over and over I would not take no for an answer ... and I think I simply just wore him down because he sat down and taught me one simple effect.

Ever since then I have been hooked and have dedicated my life to the art of magic. I now stand here nearly fifteen years later as a multi-award-winning magician. Over the years I became one of the youngest performers of the Magic Castle in Hollywood, California (performing at the age of seventeen in a twenty-one-and-older club.) By the age of nineteen, I was performing in Las Vegas, Nevada, at venues at major hotels. I was recently awarded the Siegfried and Roy Masters of the Impossible Award for the "Most Up and Coming Magician." The Society of American Magicians awarded me the title of the "Newcomer of the Year." And there is still more to this story; every three years, there is a competition known as the Federation of International Societies of Magic in which 150 contestants from over forty-seven countries compete for magic's highest honor. And on July 26, 2003, I was awarded the title the Grand Prix World

Champion of Magic. Only three Americans in the history of magic have held this title! I now have joined with the names of World-Famous Close-up Magicians and World-Famous Stage Magicians.

I am now twenty-three years old and currently touring the world performing all over Europe and Asia. I have had the privilege of performing on numerous international television programs. And, recently, I actually had the honor of performing for royalty as I just returned from performing for the royal family of Monaco. My love for the art is growing every day, with no ending in sight! I hope my continued success is no illusion. The funny thing is – to think this all started because I literally ran into the right person at the right time.

Did They Get Lucky?

A Smile Shared by Friend Bonnie Shubb …

My husband and I were relaxing in the pool on a Caribbean luxury liner. We loved to take cruises. We had been on the ship for two of our seven-day cruise. We were totally relaxed, sipping cold rum drinks with a little umbrella and lots of calories. The night was clear, and we were listening to the water hitting the side of the ship in a consistently rhythmic pattern. Then another couple came in to join us. We introduced ourselves and discovered that they were one of the many newlyweds who were on the ship celebrating their honeymoons.

The wife spoke first. "You'll never believe what happened to us," she said. "The limousine that was supposed to take us to the airport in Los Angeles got lost on the way to pick us up from our wedding reception. So, we arrived at the airport late and missed our flight."

"Gee," said my husband, "I'm sorry you went through that."

The new-groom added: "So then, when we finally arrived in Miami, the cruise ship had already left, so they suggested we fly to St. Thomas to pick up the ship. We did, and we were halfway to the dock when we were held up. All our cash was taken and all of our jewelry, except for my wife's wedding ring."

"Omigod!" I exclaimed. "I'm so sorry that happened!"

Then, the bride continued: "We finally got on board about midnight last night and got settled in our cabin. This morning we came out to the pool and were swimming. You won't believe this, but my wedding ring came off and was lost in the pool!" She was practically in tears as she related the story. Her husband hugged her. "At least we have each other – through good times and bad – we are together."

My husband and I looked at each other. We didn't know what else to say. They seemed to be trying to keep positive, but I felt so sad for them.

Suddenly, there was a cloudburst and it started to rain. My husband whispered to me – "Honey if there ever was a place for lightning to strike, it will be on this couple. We'd better get out of this pool!"

The next day we saw the same couple at breakfast, and I smiled as I saw them happily chatting with another young couple.

"You're not going to believe what happened!" called out the young woman we had met the night before. I shivered and thought, "What now?" but I didn't say a word. "Well, after you left the pool last night, we also left and changed clothes and went into the casino. We bet on the roulette table using our wedding day as the number—and it came up! 38 to 1 odds!" she bubbled. We won a lot more than the cash we had lost. Then, when we returned to our cabin, there was a message to call the purser. They were cleaning the pool filter and found my ring!"

Her husband reached over and hugged her. "See," he said, "We have each other in good times and bad – we are together!"

People?!

Oh, the swimming pool looked so inviting. I paid the admission price upon entering and even noted the "rules" on the sign. Proper attire, caps, no running, and … quiet. A place to unwind in New Zealand for a day from travels and geared to leisure, relaxation. Comfortable lounge chairs, the spacious sundeck, and even the scent was appealing. I was leading a group of teens on that day that we all looked forward to. An ideal place to wade, float, swim laps, or simply unwind. Perfect!

Not! We enjoyed the day for a total of maybe eleven minutes. Suddenly some people appeared, loudly, to advise me that they do not like teens nor want them at "their" pool. I couldn't believe my ears or eyes and the "quiet" rule was somehow forgotten. What to do? We were there – just like anyone else. I didn't want the chaos to escalate and was more stunned than anything. (This was supposed to be a perfect day!)

So much for welcome to New Zealand! I know there are people of all kinds anywhere we go in this world. This, though, was unpredictable, uninviting, and exasperating. The teens became silent and watched … when suddenly a stranger came rushing up to me. Oh no! She had observed all, and we had a brief conversation in which she informed me that is not how New Zealanders act and gave me her card. She said if she could help in any way as there is a love for New Zealand that visitors ought to experience. "Kiwis" – are an easy-going people she explained, "A country with vast wilderness, nature, and the quiet life."

We left the area and sometimes the best plans just do not work out. Exploring New Zealand, it did share the beautiful landscapes and rich culture. We explored farms and specialized sheep shearing. The live-action working dogs fascinated me. Impressive – Such control of hundreds of sheep and then splashing into a pond of water as a reward.

The journey continued. Always an experience in any travels! A year later Michael was traveling to Australia and New Zealand. I found that card. Her name was Joy. Michael sailed to New Zealand and contacted her when he reached that part of the world. You never know … Joy invited Michael to come to meet her while in New Zealand. And, that he did, and for a short while he became part of the family. They shared their island country world and Michael did more than sightsee. He helped to cut lumber and odd jobs while tasting the foods and daily life.

I even like her name. This woman came out of nowhere to bring a little world peace. The books I author all have the word "Joy" in the title. So, maybe, she was meant to be?

We have kept in touch for many years. (I had only met her for maybe a total of five whole minutes.) Joy was in the United States briefly and spent a night in my home. We talked forever … and that is what life and travel and reaching out are all about. She is way in her eighties now and on Facebook always sharing whatever she is up to.

Sometimes there is a "hiccup" and things go awry. Those can end up being the experience of a lifetime! Serendipity is one of my favorite parts of travel.

Nothing New?

"Why do you cruise? Cruising would be so boring. Anyway, once you go on one cruise, they would all be the same. Nothing new." People say that over and over. I listen. Little do they know.

Alaska is a special place for me. I have shared it with my mom, my son, and Dave. The wilderness is unexplainable. Vast forests, fjords, coastline, rivers, gold, totem poles, salmon ... and nicknamed "The Last Frontier." I have walked in sunshine and clouds, light rain, heavy rain, storms, and various pathways this way and that.

Alaska scenery is stunning and the wildlife is indescribable. Juneau is an attraction with many possibilities. It is the capital, and you cannot drive there from anywhere. In a mere six minutes though you can ascend in a tram to the top of Mt. Roberts. One time amidst heavy rain, we floated higher and higher with little to no visibility amidst thick puffy white clouds. The view once at the top is like a picture postcard, like no other and the question is which direction to glance first. One can't discover Russia on that high mountain peak, though just knowing of the Bering Strait and that Alaska was once part of Russia is history in itself.

I could write a whole book just about picturesque Alaska and the fresh air that one breathes in. Without even trying, you leave behind any worries or thoughts and observe nature at its best. Salmon jumping, flowers abloom, the flight of birds migrating, often singing, and a peacefulness wonder.

I saw mountain goats askew, almost moving sideways on the ice. We observed a brown bear up ahead on a path and the cubs wandering here and there. Bald eagles with their tremendous wingspan are right there before your eyes. I did not know until I reached Alaska that they turn white with age, just like us, though we do not like to admit it.

I would like to share two unexpected Alaska moments to always remember on my "boring" cruises. Ha! The first was Dave and I bundled in our multiple layers and scarves as the wind howled and we walked a path of exploration. I stopped to peek at the vision of greenery, assorted plants, and blooming colors sprouting everywhere. Something moved. It was significant enough to make a rustling noise as the lengthy blades of grass seemed to swish in the wind. A medium-sized something was definitely there, and we opted to distinguish what it was. We stopped in our steps and waited, watched.

It wobbled. Something? A creature I had not observed before. It seemed short and stocky, kind of roundish, and the eyes were looking right at us. It looked soft, maybe fluffy. And we realized it is not always so soft and fluffy, for it was a porcupine! Needle-like quills overlapped and protruded yet did not look long nor sharp. Cute? Moaning like noises. Maybe a "handle-with-care" type of creature not to cuddle? Amazingly, we noticed that porcupine while walking the few blocks between the ship and downtown Juneau.

Not a bear nor a bald eagle, not a caribou nor an orca, and not salmon spawning in the stream. No, a porcupine was undoubtedly something I had never before encountered in all my trips to Alaska.

Surprises can happen in any direction.

A bitter cold stormy miserable day in Juneau was another day. We had been there several times before yet always the philosophy – no two days are ever alike. The wind blew and snow fluttered. I actually trembled while carefully walking the sloshy path. Kayaks and whale watching excursions had been canceled and bear tracks noticeable yet no bear in sight. One of those days!

The Mendenhall Glacier glistened, and earthy colored wildflowers blew in the gusts of wind. One-of-a-kind flora was a sight to see shimmering with specks of fresh fallen snow and morning dew. Though such a dismal day, the surrounding colors became unbelievably vivid, and the dazzling ice gave additional astounding hues of blue. Glaciers move in their own time, freezing and melting as ice descends. Always distinct and a spectacle to witness.

Yes, Alaska's Juneau, a place I have visited almost yearly. On this day though inclimate weather was more than usual and soaked paths funneled by melting dirty water were slippery to walk on. Arriving on a cruise ship the minutes and hours of the day in port are minimal. The shuttle to get us to Mendenhall came on time and was easy so we had no worries about our return shuttle to the ship. At the breakfast buffet that morning we could see the crowd and hear a building murmur ... why get off the ship if the weather seemed so iffy. Whatever! Just seems that if you travel all that way, there will be something to see and experience.

We finished our exploration and return to the wonder of glaciers and enjoyed the environment and all it has to offer. However, in observation of reality, we could easily see how the glaciers' retreat is evident. Changes in landscape and vegetation are real. Areas that were impressive once of breathtaking majestic white glaciers with cascading waters appeared brownish and barren. Climate change!?

The bitter cold stormy miserable day was even an eye-opener as always. This time, a chance to view the retreat and reshape of glaciers and the hues of blue of the ice appearing almost mystical.

We returned to the shuttle shack to hide under a makeshift roof for shelter from chill and rain where we waited ... and waited. Hopefully watching the road for a shuttle to appear to our rescue, we heard a bit of a sound. A quiet noise seemed to get louder ... and quite curious. As we looked up, we could not believe our eyes. There in the eves was an egg, slowly, gradually cracking open. Like a circular motion and tiny cut, a hole, and a ... push. We could see the little legs pushing, stretching and a beak as a peck, peck, peck, squeak, chirp was happening. Nature. Hatching

… a tiny little fluffy chick chipping out of an egg for us to eyewitness. The top part slowly split open like the blossoming of the petals of a flower. The precious baby bird was still sitting in the bottom half of the newly cracked egg and its fluffy head was fully out. Right before our eyes! Nature was truly taking place.

A day of all days to always remember. The joy of travel. The little chick would somehow explore its new little world. Something was indeed new.

Go for It!

He watched every morsel he ate and drank. A man I met on a cruise was so worried about gaining an ounce that he did not loosen up to experience the food or the fun. Cruise lines pride themselves on the quality of the cuisine as well as the atmosphere. Order one entrée or another and experiment, try specialty tastes that might surprise you. The rotating menu of delectable favorites is plentiful, so the perfect time to experiment with different options, and the presentation can be stunning. As far as gaining weight, my mom always told me that if you take the stairs and not the elevator, you will not gain weight. And, I think there is something to that advice.

This fellow, Randy, did not taste dessert nor try any new appetizers nor entrees. He ate minimally and was there observing more than partaking. I don't care for sweets, yet I taste them just to know what others are describing. My friend Cathie always orders the "Special." That is a gooey rich chocolaty mousse masterpiece artfully designed on the plate. I tried that and a special soufflé, and other things too. I don't feel great when eating sweets, but a taste is fun and keeps me in the know. The art of it all is creative and masterful, the culinary elements coming together to create innovative appealing dishes arranged with design and color.

And – then came night number 6! There was a change, a transformation on that evening. Randy decided to stop counting calories and content and to revel in the entire experience. The waiter and busboy enticed him and happily served Randy his prime rib and ... a side taste of the fettuccine ... Yorkshire pudding ... and lemon meringue pie. Suddenly his eyes seemed to sparkle as he described the flavors, tastes, and texture in his realization that maybe, he indeed had been missing something. He became fun to dine with. He became a changed person, and I don't think he even gained weight. He did gain the experience of trying new things!

Romances at Sea

One of the more exciting moments I have witnessed while cruising happened unexpectedly. The cruise director was speaking on stage and invited a passenger up to participate in an activity. (The cruise director also held his breath after he did so.) You see, the man talked energetically into the microphone speaking to a standing-room-only audience, and did what many romantics only dream of. He got down on his knees. With a smile from ear to ear he turned to his girlfriend sitting in the audience and said, "Will you marry me?" This was a complete surprise to her, the cruise staff and almost 1500 passengers who held their breath as she gasped, took a deep breath, and said, "YES."

I was among many who had tears. Emotional, heartwarming, and how many times do we witness such surprise and the pure joy of others? Dave and I somehow soon found ourselves in the same elevator with the newly engaged couple. Beaming and radiant she told us, "I had no idea!" Her ring sparkled as it reflected into the glass of the elevator. He explained, "I always said if I ever had money to buy a ring I would propose. She was tired and went to sleep early last

135

night so I explored the ship and found the casino." He had been one busy guy; lucky at cards, paying a visit to the onboard jewelry shop, keeping the secret, and a ring, to himself all day.

They got out of the elevator looking for help to find a phone connection to call home and a buzz of excitement filled the ship that night.

◆ ◆ ◆

And on another cruise in the dining room ... Dave requested a table just for two one night to have a special evening together. The cuisine that we had was excellent. The other table for two, however, was a little close to ours, almost connected. So, romantic, yet not so private.

A cute young couple was seated next to us. We said hello and chatted briefly so as not to interfere and to have a little privacy too. They finished their dinner as we were just beginning our second course. When their dessert menu came the gal informed her boyfriend and waiter that she had enough. "No dessert tonight please!" She started to stand up and the boyfriend connivingly told her that he was looking forward to a sweet dessert. What to do? It almost seemed like an argument was looming. So much for our intimate experience, we tried to ignore it all.

The next thing we knew he nervously jumped to the floor and was almost in Dave's lap. Then, a proposal began. We could see the tenderness in their eyes and feel the magic of the moment. We looked at each other and smiled and tried to make a quick graceful escape out of the dining room. We so hoped she would agree, and we thought it should be a private and special moment just for the two of them.

◆◆◆

Cruising is in my blood! My parents are now gone, though their story always lingers on. When young, my mom went on voyages with her dad (my grandfather) for business. She looked young and he said she could be "16" to travel with him every year. Mom enjoyed the voyage and the ambiance as well as the seas. She discovered the lounge to hear music and relax in the evening. That happened to be where uniformed ship officers congregated and it was said they couldn't let a woman sit there and not dance. And dance she did. She also noticed my dad, they shared glances, although otherwise he never even acknowledged her.

The cruise had completed and reached the home port. However, it was when she was disembarking, that he asked her for her phone number. As the story goes, she asked him, "Why? You never even asked me to dance." He persisted and she did though give him her number. Whew! The rest is history. It did begin the romance of two incredible people I loved to call my parents.

They were happily married for many wonderful enduring years. For their twenty-fifth anniversary, my brother and I gave them a surprise party complete with the reaffirming of their vows. And of course, the retelling of how they met!

Gail's "New" Clothes?

"I have ……..," and stunned, I found I could not say the words. So, I tried again, "I have NO …"

I could almost not say it amidst my shock, surprise, and dismay.

"I HAVE NO CLOTHES!"

There, I said it in a quiet, subdued international hotel lobby environment in Japan. I got the words out, finally, with clearly a lot of expression. Nevertheless, I was in a place where no one understood what I was saying. The individuals I was attempting to converse with smiled with friendly knowing looks and eagerly responded in perfect English, "Thank you very much." I looked upon them questioningly and this time they bowed and actually repeated a little louder in case I had not heard, "THANK YOU VERY MUCH!" Those were among the few English words that they spoke daily.

It was that very morning, in Osaka, Japan, that I had disembarked from the cruise ship. I meticulously followed every direction from the cruise director, "Have your luggage outside the cabin door before 2 AM and apply only your appropriate azure blue tags for proper identification."

My travel companion, Cathie, and I, (in our bathrobes as we were getting ready for the gala farewell evening,) had done all of that. We meticulously each placed our clothes out to be worn the next morning, tagged our luggage appropriately, and together struggled as we pushed the enormous suitcases out through the narrow cabin door. A loud, s-l-a-m, was the abrupt noise heard near and far, when our security cabin door locked tightly with our keys inside.

It seemed like forever, and being the guest speaker on the ship, I did not feel it appropriate to navigate myself in my mini robe to the purser's station on mid-ship. For it was there those hundreds of passengers (many of whom had been in my audiences) were gathered for the traditional, astounding, champagne waterfall, toast, and captain's farewell.

No one was in the halls. Just colorful balloons placed throughout the days of the cruise, that appeared on doors celebrating birthdays and anniversaries. Some that were still inflated swayed, and the deflated balloons sagged to their own distinct movement. A dream cruise was ending, and we could do nothing other than sit ... on the floor. A passenger rushing by came within our sight, then stopped his quick pace doing an about-face to inquire as to why we were sitting on the floor in our robes. Mission accomplished! Help was soon on the way! Next, we heard the beeps of a walkie-talkie and the paced footsteps of a staff member who came to our rescue. Once he heard our tale of woe, he promised he would return soon with a passkey.

I thought that was the most entertaining and unusual tale to bring home to tell of this voyage to fascinating destinations. Once dressed elegantly and moving to the music and excitement in the atrium ascending seven decks, the last night of the cruise brought one final picturesque sunset, and the good-byes.

The next day when I exited down the long ramp and disembarked the ship, there were rows and rows of suitcases of every shape and size. I correctly identified my enormous, bulging black suitcase, noting my name, precisely printed, just as instructed, on the azure blue tags. The porters, unknowingly, picked up and moved … the wrong suitcase. The harbor transport next whisked me away to a traditional Japanese hotel in the city.

Now, my plan for that evening was to take a relaxing shower on what was the first hot day of the season and, my first day on land in weeks. I did that. A quiet night seemed particularly appealing to me because the next day I was to be the keynote speaker giving an all-day seminar in Japan. It was when I was going to put on something casual for a relaxing dinner downstairs in the hotel that I realized I had a problem. You see, when I opened "my" suitcase, it contained only an assortment of finely tailored bow ties, white stiffly starched shirts, and some elegant, custom-made … extra-large, men's tuxedos!

I was impressed with the fine threads the tuxedos were made of and I held one up for me to see in the mirror. My international speaking on the topic of creativity ... could it be done in a tuxedo?! Hmmm. It would really take more than originality and imagination, for the tuxedo was of a size that two of me could fit into it. I delved deeper into the suitcase and there was nothing even close to petite. (I pondered and thought I could possibly wear one of the heavily stiffly starched, extra tall, incredibly long, white shirts with deep pleats and black onyx buttons as ... a dress.) With, a colorful bowtie, of course!

Not knowing what else I could do, I put on my long flowing elegant floral dress with the countless tiny decorative buttons all the way down the front that I had worn for the gala farewell activities and previously declared dirty, very dirty. I ran down the hall to find Cathie. I rapidly knocked on her door, which she opened, bewildered, asking why I was once again, wearing that dress. Though I was speechless at the time, the tears flowed down my cheeks from pure laughter. I could not stop. Besides, what else could one do? Travel is full of adventure and surprises. No two days or experiences are ever the same! Travel could be defined as flexibility and, not always knowing ... what tomorrow will bring.

The reason I had no clothes was that two suitcases had been unintentionally and unknowingly switched. The efficient hotel valet in the impressive uniform with the perfect hat had lugged the heavy suitcase through the lobby, into the elevator, and to my hotel suite. When I tried to partake in the confusion and an interpretation as to what had occurred, he, over and over again, explained that, yes, he had taken my suitcase up to my room. How does one begin to communicate that I knew that, and it wasn't his fault? It was just the wrong person's suitcase, and I did not know where was my luggage?

Other guests in the lobby observed and eventually to some extent understood my predicament. With three sets of travel dictionaries and a book of Japanese phrases, the hotel staff was sketchily informed of what to them was a true dilemma and … unbelievable. Calling the cruise line headquarters was an episode too since their headquarters are in California and the time difference was of hours and … a day. Somehow, some sense was made out of the situation. Confusion? An international catastrophe? Tourists' cell phones of every melody and sound began noisily ringing as well as the phones behind the hotel desk. Not totally really understanding all of what was going to happen, the next thing I knew, a cab was hailed for me.

I was taken by surprise as the doors of the cab automatically swung open wide. (Never stand too close to a cab in Japan!) I got in and just like a wild, staged chase scene in a movie, wildly speeding through dark windy streets and turning this way and that, this was reality, and we arrived. For $35, U.S. currency, the cab driver drove me to the port of Japan. Hurriedly because I had to be there before the stroke of midnight!

I never imagined that the sight of a cruise ship could be so thrilling! We arrived amongst workmen and crew members speaking quite a few dialects and languages who were standing on the dark dock for the last minutes before the ship was to set sail. Conveyor belts were slowing as the abundance of food and supplies had filled the ship for the cruise about to commence.

I could hear the grind of the wheels and gears while racing down the platform and I caught the eyes of observers, all ... watching. And, right then and there, down the gangplank, came my suitcase. I never thought there was as much as the possibility to ever see my suitcase again. Now, in front of me, was my enormous black suitcase, with the correctly placed, azure blue tags. The ship whistles blew, and I retained the cab driver, who I know thought I was doing something illegal, to take me back to where our cab journey had begun, for yet another $35. This time, though, it was already past the stroke of midnight. There was no hurry. The switch over of the suitcase had already taken place!

I will always remember the goofiness and splendor of that journey! And – the view of the ship almost smiling/winking at me when my eyes were last upon her!

Confession: My husband still tells the story of being all the way across the world and me calling in the middle of the night on a very static phone saying, "I have no clothes!" (He stayed calm, though in his voice I could tell it was not the call he wanted to hear.)

360°

Along with the strumming of the ukulele, an exquisite multi-colorful Hawaiian lei was placed over my head symbolizing my first step into Hawaii. The lei is a symbol of welcome and the greeting is given out of friendship and honor.

My image of Hawaii was always that of colorful vivid blue waters, swaying green palm trees, lush gardens, and tranquil skies. I find Hawaii inspiring with every sunrise and sunset. There is a sense of connection as there are smiles and a friendly "Aloha" spirit. Hawaii feels like a paradise.

Volcanoes continue to reshape the earth. Diamond Head in Oahu is a Hawaiian landmark that is a backdrop to Waikiki Beach. The trail is rugged with panoramic views that Michael and I shared hiking on my second visit to Hawaii. The extinct crater was described by 19th-century sailors who thought they discovered diamonds on the slopes of the crater. Those who live there describe the colors of Diamond Head by the reason of rainfall and nature. (Rainy months gleaming shades of green and brown by summer.)

There is a scent from the abundant blooming flowers. I have a vivid recollection of shimmering plants with a variety of colors of Hawaii. I think of Hawaii as a sensory experience. Aside from the picturesque images of alluring beaches and illuminating blues of Hawaii, there is culture, tradition, and history.

Humpback whales have captured our curiosity and vision seeing them in their circular migratory cycle. Roaring waterfalls are breathtaking and often even a daily "rain" is magical. Food culture is fresh with a tapestry of eateries, flavors, and tastes. I still cannot pronounce "Humuhumunukunukuapua'a" the Hawaiian state fish. Can you? (When offered a free dinner if I could, I still could not do it.)

Dave and I encountered unusual salt in our savory Hawaiian dining experiences. Traditional Hawaiian table salt, called Alaea Salt, is an unprocessed salt that is rich in natural seawater minerals. It fascinated me. Even the salt was colorful! The color of reddish-brown, almost a sparkling glitter like orange. We found some in a little curio shop to take home as a souvenir.

In my mind, if I close my eyes and remember Hawaii, it is of the brightest vibrant oranges with bursts of blazing yellow, brown, and red that I witnessed one night in Hawaii from the deck of the ship. Lava was spilling into the ocean. The captain turned the ship 360° for views like I have never imagined. An evening with glowing lava.

Creation = lava somehow creating new land as it pours into the sea. Oozing into the sea, an oceanic volcanic eruption is a visual one's eyes witness and can hardly believe. To maneuver the vessel for changing its path, the depth of the water and the weather must be suitable – a quite different phenomenon than that of turning a car. (Remembering my dance training, discovering how to turn and spin, to perform a pirouette took balance and technique.) A pirouette can be spectacular. The leg and body and turn are all executed in a rhythmic precise way.

As you embark on a cruise journey, sailing the ocean is an adventure, if lucky enough to be on a ship turning 360° it is an unforgettable exploration of the dynamics of nature taking place. On this actively forming coastline, a kaleidoscope emerges of tilts and angles, patterns of twists and turns. Walking from bow to stern and around all sides on the open deck featured a continuous view that was ever-changing minute to minute.

Hawaii has a majestic coastline. Added was some music to accompany and heighten the mood and ambiance as the ship slowly turned and passengers walked circling the outer decks. Experiencing drama – a "tour" in the darkness of nightfall. We witnessed astonishing lava viewing firsthand as streams of lava entered the sea in a unique occurrence in nature.

The spectacle of the volcano in recent years has been unpredictable involving ever-changing locales of volcanic flow. Houses and towns sadly have been lost when she erupts, damage affecting lives. Nevertheless, island life continues.

Leaving our Hawaiian cruise, we had such special memories of so much. While in port the night in

Oahu, I received a memory to cherish. A young student of mine, Cindy, once in second grade, is now a beautiful creative woman who lives on the island, and we had just somehow connected on Facebook. We planned to meet at a resort near Diamond Head. It had only been about 46 years since I last saw her. Her smile drew her to me as she entered a far terrace overlooking the ocean as the sun was beginning to set. That night she placed a lei over my head, and I could feel the genuine love.

Now for a confession about my mistake with my fascination with the characteristic salt of Hawaii. I thought the zest and uniqueness would complement my cooking when we returned home. Uniformed airport security seemed to think differently as they rushed to an alert regarding my carry-on and me! Everything was emptied out and special officers with devices went over everything. They took samples and something lit up as they looked for contraband. The investigation was a delay, yet I did make the plane. Dave and I took a deep breath and thought it another cruise adventure! And, we did get a salty tale out of it.

Tricks of Travel

I can't tell you how many minutes and hours when traveling that I have been on a mission to find the best memento for Michael who was quite young. I learned about finding souvenirs from places afar. You name it, I brought it home. Things that reflected the culture and life of people, towns, and countries. And so, I, at last realized, a young boy who looks to see what you brought for him, wants the familiar of whatever he is into.

So, before sailing on one Caribbean cruise, I went to the popular local toy store and purchased a toy tractor, dump truck, and assorted construction vehicles. (Quite heavy if they were to come home packed in weighed luggage for sure.) I placed them all in the trunk of my car … until I reached home from my cruise that is. Michael was excited to have the trucks that little kids dream of. And, I did it again … the next trip.

Bikini Packing Put into Perspective

I was trying to figure out which bikinis to take while struggling to keep my luggage to a minimum. I was probably spending more time on this than needed. My young son, Michael, was watching and looked at me like this was a no-brainer. He simply said, "why worry, they are only the size of a pair of socks!" So, at that moment of perfect clarity, I packed a few of my bikinis (maybe 5) and smiled.

Too Much

In my teaching as well as in speeches, I encourage parents to be in touch with their children. Sometimes parents travel a lot and young children do not realize that it takes days for mail to be delivered. Especially, from faraway places, such as across international borders.

I have suggested pre-writing notes or letters and having a friend or neighbor mail them locally, so the children get mail while you are cruising. They have the delight of getting mail delivered to them while also seeing your familiar handwriting and feeling the connection.

One father thought it was a great idea. He pre-wrote cards, and it was all arranged for them to be mailed and delivered to his children. His young son came to school one day thrilled to receive a card from Daddy. Together we read the card out loud to share with all his classmates. (I can remember this like it was yesterday.) It was one of the few times that I could hardly control myself from wanting to laugh right out loud. The card said:

Dear son.

I am having a great time on this cruise. Everything is new and different, and there are so many stories to share when I come home. I have tasted delicious chocolate cake, cinnamon rolls, homemade ice cream, pizza with extra cheese, lobster, and whatever I want at the buffets. I cannot button my pants or the jacket. Picture what I look like with my buttons starting to … pop! I have a problem. I ate so much good food that my tuxedo will not fit. I knew the food would be great, but it is all so amazing. I will bring pictures and know that I love you so much.

Love, Daddy

Just the visual for me was so funny. A clever and creative dad he was. What fun he had composing that note and I teased him so when he returned home. Of all things to write, his buttons popping! He did write and connect with his kids. And they got it the next day. They were too young to figure it out and a letter from Dad or any far-away parent is always the best.

Push and Tush

Push …

People pushed into the neat orderly line we were in at LAX. The anticipation of travel and boarding an airplane was unexpectedly altered, changed to what came to be chaotic. Was this the beginning of our relaxation and island escape?

The British island with Horseshoe Bay Beach, the underground lakes, and caves awaited us as well as the colorful sands and brightly painted colonial buildings. It was only an hour earlier we had spoken to well-wishing friends with their bon voyage call. We chatted about flying to New York and then cruising to Bermuda. In our minds was the anticipation of calmness and cruising calm waters. We met Jeff and Marcy on a previous cruise and wished they could have joined us on our voyage. They spoke of commitments and why unfortunately they could not join us on our adventure.

We could not believe it! Ouch! I was literally pushed by two rude people cutting in line. In the crowd, in disgust, I opened my mouth and started to say something until I stared into their eyes. Unbelievable. It was them! Jeff and Marcy revealing their plane tickets, identical to ours. They had called on route to the airport to dissuade us from any suspicion.

And so, it was, cruising with friends was an unexpected fun adventure and an encounter to long remember. They had booked not only the same flight from Los Angeles to New York but also the very same cruise to Bermuda.

The story does not end there though. After eight days and experiences shared, we said good-bye with smiles and hugs and hopes to meet up for future times to share. We hailed a cab to a hotel for three days in New York … and … they pushed in the other side of the taxi to go with us. We could not believe it! They also had the same New York adventure!

New York after a cruise can be amazing. After all, as the saying goes, New York, New York! Not! For, to tell the truth, luxury hotel or not, at the stroke of midnight we stood downstairs in the lobby asking for … toilet paper. Being spoiled on a ship set us up to splendor, being in a hotel during the New York hotel strike can be insane. And it was!

A Holiday Like No Other

There is nothing like a cruise ship with the captivating holiday burst of color, lights, and intrigue of decorations. Walking on the dramatic decks can be an eye-opener with embellished banisters and hallways of ribbons and garland, tinsel, lights, sparkle, and shine. Deck the halls on a ship includes the atrium soaring, towering high above with winter wonder. "Elves" hang ornamental shimmering surprises from walls, halls, railings and suddenly they create falling snow sprinkling down the atrium. (Some fascinated wide-eyed children might touch and see "snow" for the very first time.) Often lights are synchronized to magical music and festivities include multi-generational celebrations.

Ahhhh ... the magic of a holiday on a cruise ship. To some it is nostalgic, and several plan a holiday cruise specifically for the feeling of merriment. Whatever holiday you celebrate, it is suddenly just like only seen in the movies, only "real."

A True Dilemma!

I boarded a holiday cruise, and the ship was its ordinary wonderful, though noise began permeating because the ship was not decked out in holiday decorations. No wreaths or elegant embellishments, no twinkling menorah, nothing to turn heads to in the atrium or beyond. NO winter paradise!

The captain explained that the previous cruise had extraordinary rough harsh stormy seas. Delays and challenges rippled causing problems stemming from the weather. Therefore, it was not safe to maneuver the ship to reach containers in Asia that store the favorite holiday decorations. (We did hear word of a few claiming "mutiny" asking how can a holiday cruise not be adorned and decorated?)

Transformation and the Best Time for Me! (And, Others)

Ta-da … I believe it is called making the best of a situation, actually a shift of anticipated holiday décor. It was more than the best – it was an unsurpassed exceptional night for me! We became amused curious mischievous elves (heroes) spilling materials while having a jolly time creating the holiday ambiance "necessary" on a cruise ship. So much work and … fun! An almost all-night experience as we helped to transform a bare ship into an unusual, extraordinary winter paradise.

Try to picture the determination and sharing of ideas amidst chuckles and roaring laughter to spruce up barren artificial trees. (Heartfelt and unique – we might even have gone overboard in our decorating.) Doilies make snowflakes as do the ones we cut like paper dolls. (Though some did get cut off in the wrong places if you know what I mean.) Smushed cotton creates beautiful snow. Paper clips and a wine cork makes clever ornaments as do corks glued together to make wreaths. Colorful paper placemats cut into chains were looped and twisted together. And the ultimate decorations of all – Combine a needle and thread + popcorn. As you might imagine, popcorn has since never been the same for me. The most hilarious, clever, and weird lopsided garland produced from the stringing of popped popcorn draped the trees.

Nothing perfect, creative handmade wonder and one of a kind = A prosperous season to all!

◆ ◆ ◆

Holidays are about the shared experiences of spending time with family and friends. Festive is the word and a colorful décor often bursts with special vibes and the celebration of it all. Holidays are warm-hearted including the memories and the way things are supposed to be. It really is all about the holiday spirit.

◆ ◆ ◆

A tree or menorah can be bright, sparkly, and reflective. I remember one Hanukah on board a ship traveling with a friend who knew nothing about Hanukah. A rabbi was hosting a celebration in the lounge, so we went and were greeted with harmony and song. The rabbi was strumming his guitar singing traditional songs as a number of cruisers joined in. So many so, that the venue had to be moved to a larger lounge and hundreds followed the rabbi like a Pied Piper. Families with children brought menorahs from home of every shape and size. Participants came from national and international areas. Some spoke/sang in different languages that made a dreidel spin and menorah ceremony seem more meaningful. Though candles are not safe on a moving ship, the reflection of holiday joy was mutual with all. Collective was cheerfulness, happiness, joy, with an appreciation for an occasion filled with opportunity and sharing.

◆◆◆

Holidays are like no other ... the time of year to feel inspired and uplifted ... reaching others too ...

Cruising is a magical celebration no matter what time of year. Yet the holidays to some are lonely. The crew is so remarkable and somehow always there for us day by day. They are, though, so far away from home. Especially at the holidays it can be emotional and can cause feelings of emptiness. My fulfillment is what little I can do for the room steward and other crew members. I know it is a personal thing and they split a basic tip amount with a multitude of the crew, however, with all our cruise prep and expenses and splurging, I sit on my suitcase when packing. Why? Because I top it off by placing little things to splurge on some caring crew members. To see their surprise and delight is what makes my heart full.

Fun! At the holiday time of year especially, I leave a surprise for the room steward every day when leaving the cabin. A candy cane, hat, door decoration, stocking, small stuffed animal, or whatever. Someone far from home with an extensive work schedule, brightening someone else's holiday is a celebration. (And Halloween it was pumpkins and ghosts and a few tasty spooky treats.) Immerse yourself in the true spirit of any holiday season. Think about it. It makes a difference!

◆ ◆ ◆

We appreciate the champagne fountain, a gala balancing tradition in a ship's atrium. I reflect also on an atrium being the place to be for a different gala balancing tradition. Cruisers of all ages gather together for traditional gingerbread house festivities of decorating and making a mess while of course tasting a lot of ingredients including gumdrops and peppermint, gooey frosting, and gingerbread. The sweet irresistible smell of peppermint and spiciness of gingerbread puts one in a festive mood. Included, of course, is noisy rambunctious giggling as the walls of gingerbread tumble down, icing oozes and drips, and all have to be put back together again.

◆ ◆ ◆

I live two off-ramps from the Ronald Reagan Library. Their annual festive Round the World holiday tree exhibit seems to speak to me. It takes place in the Air Force One Pavilion with a stunning display of trees representing 26 countries from around the world. Magical, any way you turn, twirl around, and you can appreciate distinctive traditions of near and far. This reminds me of being on a cruise ship. Hot apple cider

adds to the holiday spectacular and the inspiring decorations give a glimpse of … the world.

On Connections and Friendship

I caught a glimpse of a funicular in Valparaiso; it appeared to be a boxcar rising slowly up a sudden steep mountain. It was a tram on a cable, ascending on an incline, up, up, up. Riders experienced a mountain-scape backdrop with dramatic effects on their way to make it all the way to the top. Dave and I got into the vehicle that was shaped actually like a cage and shared this ride with other participants. Various languages were spoken in rapid sentences. (Some calm and others holding their breath.) Though we didn't communicate verbally with each other; we could see it in each person's eyes. The sight to see gliding (creeping) up the steep grade was an observation of a Chilean city and the deep-sea we had just sailed on. We did share an "ah-ha" as the vehicle bounced and bumped somewhat. Beyond dialogue – our eyes told it all.

Memories swirled in my mind of special times when I was young, days with my cherished Papa Herman in southern California. He would purchase our round-trip tickets for Angels Flight, and I can remember hopping aboard, my hand in his, going straight up, about two blocks in equivalent above L.A.'s steepest streets. As a child, I do not remember being afraid riding the funicular as much as curious and intrigued. Strangers shared the car we were in as we all gazed at the ascent to the top. I felt like we were sharing some of our town for others to experience.

My grandpa, a learned man, spoke many languages and explained to me the word funicular, did not mean "fun." He said a funicular is a track, a pulley, and an engine. The power of the engine gets the car to go up (or down) a steep incline. I heard the word funicular spoken in Latin, Spanish, and French, so different, and to this day wish I had studied many languages. We rode Angels Flight in Los Angeles, a narrow-gauge funicular, which is a historic landmark. This incline railway in Bunker Hill, Los Angeles, was no longer in service when I last stopped by. This architectural star has appeared in mysteries and multiple television shows and movies over the years. (From Perry Mason to recently, La La Land.)

Oh, how I marveled at the creativity and colors of the steep hills in Valparaiso, Chile. Riding the funiculars amidst clifftop dwellings I observed quirky art and seaside dramatic views. Known as the 'Jewel of the Pacific,' there is an artistic vibe that I wish I had days to wander and explore more of the narrow and twisting streets. The street art and murals are of a graffiti type, bursting with color and culture. Sometimes called, a "Bohemian culture."

During part of our stay, we explored the slopes, vistas, and stunning views with new friends we met on the ship, Anne, and John, from Toronto. An accomplished award-winning fabric quilt artist, Anne was so inspired that she wants to return to the atmosphere of art that surrounds one in Valparaiso. We had the opportunity a later year while on a ship to spend a day in port in Nova Scotia. Anne and John vacationed in the quaint fishing village so we could spend a day together at Peggy's Cove Lighthouse. We also did a pre-cruise travel stay with them in Toronto for a special time together. Anne made us a small one-of-a-kind custom quilt that is framed and in our entry hall. Friendships made on a cruise can be everlasting, no matter how far we live apart. It is interesting how art, places, and travel can connect us.

On the day of writing this piece, I went for a walk and met up with my neighbor, Margie, born and raised in Chile. I told her I was writing about Valparaiso. With her always laughter at my pronunciation, she had me repeat after her the name of the city and we went into her home. There hanging on her wall, she shared an exquisite colonial-era painting of Valparaiso of years past, depicting vast hills and such contrast. All, before the colorful buildings, architecture, design, and steep narrow roads as we know of it today.

Fresh seafood is available in the Valparaiso wharf setting by the sea surrounded by a labyrinth of cobbled alleyways, hills, and remarkable street art. Local Chilean food features a variety for your taste buds, each described as "homemade." They say the town is made up of 42 hills all connecting this way and that in an incoherent way. Dave and I one night meandered down the steep staircases to discover some Chilean cuisine. We passed a local market, watched the sunset, and observed fishermen displaying their catch of the day on tables set out on the sand on the vast beach.

We found a quaint small eatery with only a few tiny tables with a friendly waiter. Fresh flowers were hanging, and it seemed to us the place to be. The menu was extensive and looked interesting so we attempted to order what we thought locals would partake in. Our Spanish is not precise, and we already knew that Chileans speak many dialects with different accents.

Across the room was another small table for two covered with a hand-embroidered tablecloth. An older couple was sitting there who were watching us and later made an attempt to catch us in conversation. None of us spoke the same language! It is real though to talk to someone who doesn't speak the same language. Smiles say a lot. They seemed to radiate happiness as their faces lit up with broad grins. It was challenging and with some creativity, we shared the moment of the evening. They appeared delighted that we communicated as we did with an understanding that we were enjoying their town and traditional atmosphere and cooking.

A smile is universal. Both couples left with pleasure and a sense of joy. Us, feeling their friendship and so welcomed, and them, appreciating our well-wishes for watching them toast and the fuss of the waiter, we understood that it was their anniversary that they were celebrating that evening.

In and Out

Eleven hours and forty-three minutes. My plane from Los Angeles landed in Denmark after the long international flight. Once through with customs, passport check, and luggage claim, I proceeded to walk the lengthy hallway to find transportation to the heart of Copenhagen. I heard s-c-r-e-a-m-i-n-g ... "Gail!" It was my friend Clare flying in from Arkansas to meet up with me. Fantastic! Her plane had arrived early, and she surprisingly was there with her bright smile to welcome me. It was her first-ever European travel and actually, the very day of my birthday.

What a great way to enter a foreign country and to begin an escapade! We met in Japan ten years earlier when we were both Fulbright Memorial Scholars. We had kept in touch all this time and vowed to one day discover new experiences together. We had stumbled with our Japanese language while in Japan and now, were attempting Danish. It was in Japan when together we thought we ordered well using Japanese and even pointed to the plastic replicas of specialized cuisine. Ha! The delivery of our food was truly not anything like we thought we had ordered. (We thought we ordered thick noodles in a savory sauce. What was served, honestly, consisted of tortilla-like strips rolled resembling an enchilada with a reddish sauce.) Our memories contained a lot of shared non-stop hilarity.

Copenhagen was wonderful to explore. Bicycles and pastry are everywhere amidst museums, artistic designs, and treasures. A highlight was walking high and low, naturally getting lost, and discovering the outdoor fresh fish market. Yum! We explored crown jewels and castles and the bronze iconic little mermaid statue that really is little. My birthday, planned by Clare, was our stroll through Tivoli Gardens, a themed amusement park with gardens and ambiance. Dinner was peaceful by a scenic waterway with swans strolling and traditional Danish dishes.

We stayed in a charming boutique hotel with access to the bustling streets where we could walk nonstop. In the morning, a cozy smorgasbord breakfast was served in a picturesque patio. We wandered to an exhibition about renowned Hans Christian Andersen which featured his stories and famous fairytales that seemed to almost come to life. Interesting, Solvang, a sister city of Copenhagen, is only an hour from where I live. Of course, there too is an exhibit about Hans Christian Andersen, the storyteller of many generations.

Onward. To the ship! (Why we had come in the first place.) Each and every cruise day was an experience like no other. The ship cruised through enormous fjords going north until we could see the only tundra at the far north cape, Nordkapp. Puffins were in their native habitat after we experienced the herding of reindeer in their natural environment.

We had the opportunity to spend the morning in an ice bar in Honningsvag, Norway. We donned silly-looking silver capes and discovered everything made of – ice. The bench, the glasses, and an igloo to go into. All was a radiance of blues, plus funny to pay to get … so cold. An unbelievable "artic" experience. (One that was on my bucket list.)

A highlight was the large husky dog who greeted us and then proceeded to turn away. He hid next to a Christmas tree though it was summer. I wanted to take a picture of Lunchas, the dog who helped when the ice was dug up for the assembly of the ice bar. I was told that Lunchas was a special member of the family, and no pictures were possible since Lunchas does not like Paparazzi.

We went on a tour up to the top of a mountain via snow-blocked roads, sharp turns, and spectacular steep views. The sun glistened and the untouched snow was deep and cold. The coach made an un-expected stop for anyone who wanted to venture outside. Clare from Arkansas could only tease me, a California girl. I, of course, had to get out and at least throw a snowball. The laugh was on her as she play-fully came to join me and was the one who fell smack down in the wet soggy snow. She was unharmed, yet very wet.

So, our cruise continued with unknown, unex-pected happenings each day. Clare liked the early morning to run up to the top deck, have her smoke (Yuk) and bring down lattes for us. (Yea.) Early in the cruise she often got lost, and the room steward somehow was always there to guide her. He also surprised us with the unusual animal towels each night. (Especially the ones she loved that hung from the ceiling.)

Skipping now to the last day ... Clare wanted to do something special for the room steward. A tip? Yes. Extra? Of Course. And – unusual. Picture this, a "body" hanging from our ceiling. It featured my pirate hat with a towel face and long dangling arms and legs. The face features were carefully drawn, and the arms and legs were constructed of fifty U.S. dollars. A sight to behold! Truly. A hanging figure in our cabin. The room steward was excited as his brother was boarding from another ship that day. We turned out the lights in the cabin as we disembarked. Kind of sad as our adventure had come to an end and we each were flying home to different parts of the country. We told the steward not to enter until we were gone. Gone? We disembarked doubled over loudly chuckling to the point that others wondered what shenanigans or what we could have possibly done.

Into the trip had been a good omen the way we joined each other. Out of the trip with a treat for a well-deserved room steward and two silly friends with the happiest of memories for sure. (Wish we could have seen his face when he discovered the "stow-away" in our cabin!)

A Different Sort of Welcome

What an intriguing chance to explore Russia, the largest country in the world. Many of us went on a tour to glimpse the varied landscape and diverse culture. They took us to a restaurant designed like a log cabin. Horizontal logs interlocked at the corners. It was constructed in a rich wood that seemed rustic and interesting. An enormous stuffed brown realistic-looking bear greeted us in the entry as we walked in. One could hear the loud click-clack of sticks echoing as dancers waited for us in the dining area with live authentic music. It was exciting to be "living" the culture as the locals do. The friendly wait staff proudly informed us in their broken English that President Putin comes here. That was remarkable in itself!

And, of the food! Non-stop Russian cuisine was flavorful, savory, with a taste of homemade everything. First, came steaming hot freshly baked black bread. (That was worth the tour in itself.) Caviar sparkled on little hand-painted ceramic dishes; potato salad was sweet with a taste of pickle. People chanted various "toasts" as vodka was tasted. Each variety of vodka came in many distinct flavors and tastes. There was a unique "toast" as all stood and raised their glasses to join in the fun and taste a few. I am usually close to a "teetotaler" yet tasting the vodka with rye was remarkable. (My favorite.) It tasted almost like fresh-baked rye bread. We experienced blood-red borscht, the traditional Russian soup made from beets, cabbage, and potatoes. It was served cold with a dollop of sour cream and fresh lemon.

This meal was a feast, and we could see why President Putin would be fond of that restaurant. (If only we could meet the president!) Plates of assorted sizes were brought filled with interesting tastes and textures. More classic Russian favorites included shashlik, a kebab with a combination of vegetables and meats. Then, cute little pirozhki pastries arrived with fillings such as cheese, potatoes, and cabbage. Fluffy, fat, dumplings known as pelmeni contained different fillings, jams, cheeses, or even chocolate. They showed us that almost all of the delicacies were enhanced by adding the topping of freshly whipped butter or slivki, freshly made sour cream.

Fellow passengers dined and we couldn't decide which was best, the food or the music or lively dance. I shook the wooden click-clacks along with a kick of my feet. I thought it was fun as I like to dance, and I wanted to remember to bring the memory of this day's entire experience home to share with others. When it seemed time to leave and continue the tour, sweets were brought out that were delicious plus delightful to see. The morozhenoe was the finale of a sweet ice cream with your choice of toppings; sweet, fresh berries, and more.

Walking to the bus I bought a CD featuring music of the day that I could take home to enjoy and reminisce, though I wished I could also take home the steaming hot freshly baked black bread. I can still almost taste it! I watched a man hand painting the Russian Matryoshka dolls that stack with decreasing sizes one inside the other. I bought a set in bright red and gold with nine dolls stacked inside each other. One night on the ship I, of course, had to see for myself, and placed all 9 dolls, each bigger than the next, standing up on my bed. When the ship swayed, the dolls swayed too, and all fell down together. Great, like a puzzle, I had to figure out which was which to put them all back together again.

Those of us on the tour couldn't have been happier. A taste of Russia. When the coach made a brief stop on the way; I bought the best potatoes ever from a woman in a colorful hand-embroidered apron with a bright smile. They were white and flavored with a touch of butter and fresh parsley. I paid over the price because that is what I love to do in a foreign country when mixing with the locals. I always feel that if I am on a grand ship and exploration; I can help others who are living a life in a remote area. We hugged and she let me take a picture of her. Full as I was, yes, of course, I tasted the potatoes. Yum.

Another day, another experience like no other. The ship arrived at the small island of Kizhi. Soon I was on a coach driving among trees, nature, and the crisp air. In view was an intricate 18th-century Russian wooden church made entirely of interlocking wood, with no metal involved – not even a single nail. Indescribable.

The guide had been required to collect our visas and told us to follow him to discover a real log cabin, an example of what Russian village people spend their bitter winter in. One by one everyone followed though I thought the charming restaurant had resembled a log cabin to me. Two new friends I had made on the cruise from Chicago had the same thought as I did: "Our tour is short and why see a log cabin now?" So, we decided just to explore a little by walking to the left, rather than following the crowd to the right to see … a log cabin.

Annie, Jim, and I walked a path of brush and could hear birds chirping as the swish of trees moved in the breeze. We agreed we were happy to be away from the crowd and maybe we would wander and encounter a little village. The quiet was so peaceful.

To our surprise that calmness became confusion, bedlam. Rustic frightening-looking men with enormous machine guns started shouting at us in Russian. Hands up and frozen, we had no idea what we had done. This was not a James Bond movie; it was real, merely us, three tourists seeing what they could see. We could not speak a word of Russian and they could not, or would not, speak a word of English. Nothing happened. Whew! But, what to do? So, after a while, we slowly, yes s-l-o-w-l-y, walked a little to the left. Right before our eyes appeared different men. Actually, they were handsome and donning wool blend sport coats, only with handguns pointed right at us.

More thunderous shouts in Russian and their eyes and expression clearly told us that we were not where we were supposed to be!

We slowly moved as we changed our minds and location. They, there were many of them on all sides, watched us. We could still hear the Russian being spoken loudly a mile-a-minute and had no clue what we had done. This was not a joke, they were serious, and this was real, concerning, as our lives were at stake. The next minutes were indescribable, what was going to happen to us? Were we to be kidnapped or taken away? Far away? Too bad the crowd was just far enough away visiting a log cabin and nowhere to hear or see our very threatening predicament.

I can only say that what happened next is a moment I shall – n-e-v-e-r ... forget. We saw strange small unusually marked planes that had landed right there in the dirt. We heard the sound of the wind blowing and Russian being spoken faster than any language or dialect I have ever heard. And there before us ... couldn't be? What we saw was a man walking casually, he had a nice smile, he was wearing a casual jacket and pants, no gun in his hands, and his hair blowing every which way. It was – President Putin walking towards our path! Feeling a machine gun as tall as I was touching my – shoulders, guards stood before their President and us. We heard his words, in perfect English, "Hi. Welcome to my country."

Those planes were not aliens; they were Putin's protection and part of his security and entourage. The handsome men were his bodyguards and secret service. President Putin was quietly, quickly, ushered away to disappear out of sight. And that ... was my day on a tour in Russia!!

Chicken Soup

Dave had a moment one day where he didn't feel so good. Aha! I thought, chicken soup to the rescue. (The remedy of an "old wives' tale.") I always heard it soothes your symptoms and makes you feel better. Of course, because the last place one wants to be sick is on a cruise ship. I quickly took the stairs up to the buffet to obtain a bowl of hot broth, comfort food.

I felt good that my remedy was just what Dave needed. Little did I know I would face an unusual encounter. (Anything can happen when you least expect it). I found a tray to take the hot soup to our cabin. I stepped into the elevator safe with the soup on the tray as there would be no spills. Yes!

People in the elevator I did not know, knowingly smiled, and one man questioned what I was doing. Obvious – taking hot steaming soup to my cabin. And then it happened. The man and the woman he was with in the elevator got into a screeching argument. Louder and louder. I could not believe my ears and I was struggling to balance the soup. "You would never do that for me" was how it all began. And so, as it continued, when the elevator door opened on the next deck, I scurried off.

It then was actually a task to juggle that bowl of soup down so many flights of stairs ... Goodness! Dave appreciated the soup and in no time felt as good as new.

Windows of Opportunity

Amsterdam is lovely with canals, narrow buildings, and the incredible "window-shopping." I had been there before with memories of charm, Dam Square, the Anne Frank House, windmills, museums, and delicious espresso and cheeses. However, on this trip, I became preoccupied though with ... a dilemma.

My mom and I flew to Amsterdam for our cruise. The timing, weather, and excitement of an additional adventure together seemed to get us there quickly. However, upon our arrival, we realized that her luggage did not get there as quickly.

We took transport to the ship and became like passengers I have met on every cruise, the ones with no clothes! We filed reports for Mom's carefully packed suitcase and after numerous inquiries of the airline, were told that it did not look hopeful.

Our arrival was the weekend of Easter, and I was to learn that in Holland they celebrate Good Friday, Easter Sunday, and ... Easter Monday. The opportunity to find a shop/anything open was not possible. I did find a swanky hotel with a gift shop to purchase a warm sweatsuit for my mom. She did not usually wear sweatsuits, but it was cuddly warm, and we were there in an unexpected cold front with a wind chill besides.

Eighty-year-old Mom became happy and warm in her new clothes. Nothing was open due to the holidays. Walking in Amsterdam I discovered one of "those shops." What to do? I wandered in and the store manager was keen to help. All I wanted was … some underwear for Mom. I explained our situation and he did not blink an eye revealing to me an astounding assortment; stick-on bikini bottom, crotchless, see-through, with fringe or strings, and even "delicious" edible underthings. He must have noticed the expression on my face because he inquired as to why these were not my taste. OK, so I bought Mom one pair of their most conservative unmentionables which he wrapped in lavish classic lingerie gift-wrap with glitter and pizzazz. When Mom opened this, she good-naturedly took it in stride. Actually, we laughed nonstop. One of those moments!

The next day we went on an excursion. Mom proceeded to find a café to try their hot espresso while I walked to see a town as the cobblestones were not something I wanted her to endure. I was timely and returned to board the coach. Mom was not there! "Great," I exclaimed out loud in exasperation, "Now I have lost my mom too!" The tour guide informed me my mom was in the corner shop tasting freshly baked delicious pastry and wondered what I implied. After I found Mom and we explained to this total stranger what had happened, she kindly got on her cell phone and started making calls and talking a mile-a-minute in other languages. Before I knew it, the luggage that we were told was truly impossibly "lost" she had located. She said, "Whenever one loses luggage you always call the airline hub." Atlanta has lots of lost luggage from code-sharing airline flights. And it was so, for one and half days later, in the atrium of the ship, to our surprise, appeared Mom's luggage.

We emailed the guide after sailing to express our gratitude. The memories of travel are usually filled with the people that you meet. Her name was Vera, and we will never forget her! And you know, every trip has a window of opportunity!

Cruiser Beware

As the ship pulled into the island, the water spar-kled with the sun's reflection on the mixed hue of blues. An island of beaches, secluded coves, and tasty fusion cuisine that I remembered. Passengers out on deck watched as the ship pulled into the harbor. I was looking forward to an island day at a spot that fos-ters a stress-free vibe. There was a light sea breeze in the air as Cathie and I strolled along the boardwalk. We were parallel to the town noticing little shops just steps from the sea featuring local arts and crafts, trendy clothing, local jams, and jellies, and more.

We noticed a brightly colored small wooden beach hut with shelter overhead from the hot sun. There were some high bar stools where one could sit with cocktail in hand and toes in the sand. A place to sip a cold drink, pay attention to calypso music, and enjoy the laid-back tropical atmosphere. We each ordered a frozen drink to sip amidst ocean ambiance and this day to remember.

Being there I remembered the locale from a previ-ous trip that it was near a former royal residence. It was a charming old boutique mansion with a colorful history located on the beach boardwalk. I told Cathie I would go off to quickly take a picture to send to Lynne who had been there with me and dreams of a return.

So, I walked only a few yards away, relished the view, and snapped a few pictures of the lush landmark and grounds. I strolled back to Cathie sitting at the beach bar anxious to try my soothing cold tropical drink with a hint of coconut. My drink was there waiting for me, only next to it, Cathie was hanging half off her bar stool. Something strange/serious had happened in those few minutes. There was a sudden unexplained change. Cathie exhibited unusual behaviors and she was not herself.

Somehow with all my strength, I dragged her, literally, away from the scene. My mind raced and those in the surrounding area just continued with their jiving to the music and ocean sounds. (As if nothing had happened.) How her demeanor had changed so rapidly was frightening. Her speech was slurred, and she was … different.

I pulled Cathie away to return to the ship embarkation area. She was difficult to move seeming to know nothing and smiled – at least not resisting me. I got her to the cabin, and she seemed to pass out only to remember little when she woke up. To this day we do not know what someone placed into her drink. Similar to what we see in the movies, she was drugged, and it took immediate effect.

No, this is not a fun story to tell. It is relevant in that we are both world travelers and … it did happen to us. Sometimes on the ship, the daily news has said "do not drink anything in town that is not sealed and capped."

Obviously, they had a reason for the warning. I think the takeaway from this is – be careful. Years have gone by, and we still wonder at what exactly happened.

I do have a memory to share of when I was a young child. Many years ago, my family was in Mexico where we visited the local little stalls and shops, bought fun mementos, and took our pictures wearing an enormous sombrero while sitting on a donkey. It was warm and I wanted something cold to drink. My dad, a pharmacist, was hesitant and said NO. (It seemed to me that bottled water would be OK anywhere.) He took me around to the back and there was a long hose with a flow of water coming through from a faucet that was filling water bottles. So, the NO was not only a precaution but the reality of it all.

Travel is the best thing I know. Only … be careful … here there and everywhere!

The Man of Our Dreams

Across the main dining room appeared the most handsome well-dressed man we ever had seen. Each night, in different tuxedos or clothes worth noting, we noticed him. Curiosity on a ship? Who was he? What was the story? The wonder of it all …

Traveling with a group of five women, this was the unknown mystery to be solved. Finally, one night we walked to the other side of the dining room to meet the man of intrigue and maybe get an autograph or picture. You never know! He was seated that night at the same large round table amidst only women. He wore a dark blue blazer, with a pale blue shirt and striking tie. Fashion coordinated – like out of a magazine! Was he shy? Arrogant? With enthusiasm and gusto, we said hi and then he only stared at us. And, to our astonishment, he would not talk. Not one word.

Ohhhhhh – Because the man of our dreams was a "dummy." Not as the word might represent – a genuine inanimate being!

As we learned, it was a group of women ranchers traveling together. The mannequin was their mascot that sat beside a driver on land trips in isolated areas. With such an uncanny resemblance to a human, of course, he could not talk!

The women brought him on the trip – "just be- cause" they exclaimed. What fun when they under- stood that we had been eyeing him for days and nights. Travel stories to tell!

Curiosity of course never ends though. We won- dered how they would get him off of the ship and home on an airplane. The last night of the cruise we were silly and together wandered the halls to find out. You know, the hallways are always crammed with tagged and overstuffed luggage. After strolling several long hallways and many decks dodging the baggage waiting to be picked up, we saw it. A body bag!!!

The Little Things

Sometimes it is the little things that make a voyage the most memorable. I was craving coconut. On the ship, it was served in frosting, pudding, and pancakes. And, sometimes toasted and shredded or in exotic drinks or tangy treats. I was in Hawaii, and I could almost taste ... fresh coconut. While walking in town I could see palm trees swaying in the distance. We went on a plantation tour where locals gripped and ascended the tall coconut trees. We were not there long enough though to even have a taste. (I could not get coconuts out of my mind.)

The next day Dave and I went for a walk and found a secluded beach and shared some time alone together. As we strolled along a beach there was ... a coconut that had just fallen. A wave broke and the gentle waves washed ashore. The water lapped up on the sand and the coconut danced around. I hoped it would not get washed out to sea.

To my fortune, it stayed amidst the sand and various shells. We ran up to it as if we had discovered a genuine treasure. Oh yes! Of course, we had no tools to open the coconut. My hero became determined for me to have my coconut craving once and for all.

Dave found rocks and pieces of driftwood, and with immense effort and determination, cracked open the coconut. On that hot afternoon, with great delight, we drank the delicious rich coconut milk. Best of all, we ate the crisp coconut meat that was a culinary treat of our trip.

◆ ◆ ◆

Do you know how some things seem to somehow trigger others? Well ... writing this story got me into coconut mode. I don't have it often, however, Dave went to the store to buy the eggs for me. You see, a coconut pie somehow seemed appropriate! Cool and gray haze on what would be a "California Day" and the perfect stage for ... baking! Creamy coconut custard pie with abundant coconut flakes and brown crispy crust. It smells heavenly and I already peeked in the oven ...

Time and Place to Kiss a Fish

Slippery gushy spaghetti being thrown this way and that. Powdery fresh fine flour and raw eggs are tossed with just enough force to explode and cover observers. Weather permitting on the pool deck with excitement and silliness mounting, King Neptune arrives with his golden trident along with a graceful, lovely mermaid and an entire entourage. (Usually, the disguised cruise director, ship officers, and staff are the last you would expect to be throwing noodles.) Mock harsh treatment and embarrassment ensue. Excitement mounts as cruisers are encouraged to kiss a slimy fish or some hilarious feat.

The transformation from a slimy Pollywog is a ceremonious event. It is custom to initiate pollywogs (sailors who have never crossed the Equator) into the Kingdom of Neptune upon their first crossing of the Equator. Often just an initiation of fun insane gags and good-natured mischief. A parade, music, and transition while in the open sea. Some might call it entertaining while others think of it as a grand spectacle. Such a milestone event! (I heard a lady exclaim "I have sailed the world and I would never go on any ship that hurls damp sloppy things onto people and a ship deck. Of all things!") I guess she has not sailed to far-away places yet. This ceremony and ritual prove the cruisers are worthy of making an epic crossing as well as protecting the ship and all passengers. One might even take home an honorable ceremonious symbolic certificate actually signed by King Neptune himself. We proudly have some.

Oh no – another notable sea-faring tradition and it involves the nose! Blue noses! Painting noses blue was the highlight of all my cruising. First, I lectured in the theater about destinations and age-old traditions. Norway was the moment of exhilaration. I prepared the passengers as we were crossing the Arctic Circle. Blue noses represent the cold arctic winds and ice, as in The Order of The Blue Nose induction. This rare ceremony delves into the lore of the sea and is a colorful navigation milestone at 66°34′ N.

I guess it was being in the right place at the right time. And the honor to achieve the criteria to receive a coveted official experience and Blue Nose certificate. Exhilarating! Passengers throughout the ship came together for a unique transformational ceremony and truly a story to tell. The camaraderie of cruisers at times becomes like a family, people sharing long treasured memories. With the line crossing significance, I had the distinct honor to paint one, two, hundreds, thousands of noses to have a blueish tint. (Some said if you merely stuck your nose in the waters you would turn – blue.) Not!

Actually, I find it difficult to explain the hilarious entertaining fun of that day. Walking around a huge cruise ship swinging a bucket of blue paint and using a paintbrush with a long handle and too big bristles was unforgettable. The skeptical were soon first in line, cameras flashing and smiles wide.

People often ask me what is my favorite cruise ship? On each cruise I discover the adventure and experiences to be distinctive and memorable. The best? That depends on the crew, the staff, that truly create the flavor of every cruise experience. King Neptune's entourage and spaghetti was nothing compared to blue noses which were a feat to be had.

Seizing Opportunities

Shared by a Passenger Named Julie ...

Excited as we were about to take our Christmastime cruise in Asia, I had no idea how important that cruise was going to be to me after the fact. Taking our two boys, ages 5 and 11, on a 4-week trip from China to Cambodia was not an easy decision to make. Not just taking them out of school for that length of time, or the cost, or the public health issues, but also their ability to absorb that much information at once – all of it paled in comparison with my lifetime dream to see Angor Wat, especially the "tomb raider tomb." Logic set aside, we embarked on the expedition, made possible only by the fact it was held together by the cruise line.

It was everything we wanted and more for all of us! We got home in late December and spent the remainder of Christmas vacation going absolutely nowhere.

Once the kids got back to school from winter break it was time to catch up with all the errands, one of them being to take care of my annual physical exam. It was not the usual routine and boring thing this time around; the next thing I knew I was in surgery for bilateral stage 2 breast cancer. Strange as it may seem to some, one of my first thoughts, when the diagnosis came, was how very glad I was that we had gone on that trip, but fulfilling a lifetime dream just before receiving the diagnosis of cancer does help to blunt the edges. I am glad I went on that trip with the kids while I had my full energy and didn't put it off with thoughts of how there's always time to do it later.

Sometimes there's not.

In the meantime, as soon as I started my year of chemo, I told my husband we needed something to look forward to after my treatment is completed. We've set our sights on a cruise to Europe, another place I've always wanted to go but never have. I can't wait!

Going to the Dogs

Here is the routine – smooth arrival into the home port ... ship cleared for disembarkation. The luggage has been placed outside the cabins and already removed. At a given time, passengers can safely maneuver through stairs, hallways, and that final walk down the gangplank. After leaving the ship, U.S. citizens and non-U.S. citizens separate into two areas to show officers their travel documentation. Next is the brief check of luggage and declared merchandise by local authorities.

Truthfully, I always feel sad at the last ultimate walk off a ship. Knowing that the cruise ... is over. Yet there are always so many stories to share upon reaching home and the anticipation of the next trip whatever, and wherever it may be.

On one memorable occasion, all of the above took place as we claimed our luggage and passed through the security screening checkpoints. We showed our necessary documents, and then ... everything stopped!

The security dog sniffed once and sniffed again and made a discovery in the terminal. The canine handlers are trained to read their dog's change of behavior, and something was detected. Cruisers become somewhat of a family onboard and how curious that one of us was other than usual. The alarming canine behavior uncovered something as one gal was instantly escorted by the authorities to an isolated area. The large secure disembarkation room came to a halt. A threatening sense was noted and the urge to ask "why?"

Another unusual travel story for sure! Any essential risk was dismissed, and the cruiser was released. However, a part of her luggage was confiscated. The condition and threat were found to be minimal to others and produced a laugh plus a lesson to not forget.

Can you even guess or imagine? It was – a box of dog biscuits casually packed into a suitcase. Translated in any language – normally a treat and a yummy discovery for sure. The security dog did the task. It scored. Almost! Dog biscuit goodies including multiple flavors and sizes must have been imagined and almost tasted.

Not quite though the end of this story. We were safe this time. Dave however strongly suggested to me to certainly not pack dog biscuits in any of our suitcases! I have a fondness for animals and always packed them in my luggage. For example, Pompei and numerous cities where there are stray dogs that seem to need attention and food, let alone a tasty treat ... Traveler beware!

About a Dinner Gone Wrong

Dave reserved a dining window table just for two and I remember dressing up for a special evening. We arrived on time hand-in-hand and looked forward to a unique experience that particular night. And it was "special" in that it was different than any other of our sailing experiences. It began with an ocean view as the clouds burst with an emotional sunset of natural beauty. The colors seemed brilliant, and one couldn't look away. Staring out the window some clouds lingered, and the view was like a painting.

The menus we were handed displayed a variety of tempting dishes. The waiter was unusually brief though in giving any food descriptions or answering questions about ingredients or style of cooking. The offerings were plenty, the expansive courses enticing, and we were hungry.

We ordered appetizers and soup as a crusty hot just-baked sourdough bread was served. I had a French onion soup that was tasty and cooked with perfection. Dave had a rice noodle soup with a light flavored broth that he liked as well. My appetizer included seared baby artichokes and kalamata olives. Dave had pan-baked shrimp with Meyer lemon and a savory sauce.

A great way to begin an elegant meal. And we were curious to see (and taste) our entrees. I ordered a crusted halibut with sea salt and caramelized vegetables. Dave ordered a chicken with lentils and oven-roasted broccoli. We thought we would order our dessert when completing our entrees and then decide what was most tempting.

We waited. And, we waited. So far, we had empty appetizer plates and soup bowls in front of us resting on the white linen-covered table. And, how long could it possibly take for the preparation of our upcoming courses? Nice atmosphere, fine dining, no eye contact with dining staff, no dining staff in sight … and no more food?

We waited. Eventually, the head waiter was in sight. Progress?! Not! He made his way to the table and the message was … shocking. Timely? No, as our order had never even been placed. An apology, yes, and then the news that our waiter had … walked off of the ship.

The ship was docked for an overnight in the port in Hawaii. Some of the staff had reached the conclusion that working exceptionally long hours, seven days a week, was not for them. And, so, our waiter was indeed one of them.

So, no two days or nights or dinners or experiences are ever the same on a ship or in any travel for that matter. This was a first for us. We obviously found food elsewhere and still years later shake our heads at the thought of that "special" dinner.

Mayhem

The energy in the air. Smile – flash – photographers and filming everywhere – a magic memory.

Ahh – To be among the first passengers on a brand-new cruise ship? First to walk on the gangplank, first in the cabin, first in the venues all around the ship. To hear the "welcome aboard" from the eager awaiting crew – one could hardly wait!

The first time a ship sets sail with revenue-paying guests, there is the inaugural exuberance. The feeling of ensured splendor and something brand new. The passengers, the crew, even the locals in the port, all share bragging rights being the "first." Almost like getting in a new car for a test drive and the smell and touch of newness. No "wear and tear" on something new ... pristine condition? I was lucky enough to share the anticipation with countless others who stepped onto a gangplank greeted by the beaming faces of a welcoming crew.

It is often portrayed as a fairytale to go on a "maiden voyage." To be in on the beginning excitement with all of the thrilling gala hurrah, pennants, music, and grandeur. History!

My experience, however, on a maiden voyage out of

New York was a … catastrophe. (The ship really was not ready to sail!) I used to think … how can anyone not enjoy a cruise. I can believe it now. A mess everywhere existed as crew encouragingly said to go to the casino as a band was playing in order to find some distraction and enjoyment. When I got there, water dripped and oozed down onto the musicians who had to cease playing. Of course, we did not sink, yet one deck leaked down through to the next.

I usually am friendly and say "hi" to acknowledge others whether I know them or not. I said "how are you" to a lady as I found a poolside lounge chair to sit on. "Not good" was the reply and she continued, "My husband was stuck in the elevator." Oh?! It is arguably not a comedy – it is being on the ocean when you wish you could perhaps be anywhere else.

The friends I traveled with were not enthusiastic about cruising at all. It was their teenage daughter's cabin that they told me smelled. I thought they were just finding picky things to make their point. Returning to her cabin that evening, found that the bathroom had exploded from the round little drain in the middle of the flooring. Another family, their young 10-year-old son went to see the evening activities and proudly ordered a Virgin drink as he had seen in the movies. An hour or so later, it was truly not a "virgin drink" as he was almost green in the face and not feeling too well.

With my friends, we went to the purser first thing the next morning to find out how to disembark as soon as possible at the next port. It was not going to be possible as the dense fog was not expected to lift, and the Canadian port was going to be skipped. We felt stuck even longer.

Eventually, when all was said and done, passengers were packed and more than ready to escape this new mega-ship. It was the staff in the atrium with the final instructions, "Don't tell anyone, but we have not yet figured a system to get you off the ship." Final chaos ensued and it was sad since it was a struggle for some to get their suitcases off of the ship.

Shipboard "routines" were being launched. The magic word should probably have been – "flexible." It appeared in news headlines – and later somewhat forgotten – as was the name of that ship – that was forever changed!

Today, maiden voyages are being launched after a ship is assessed and sea trials are completed. Sea levels are measured, and worst-case scenarios studied. The ocean is powerful, so technicians, scientists, engineers, and crew strive to identify maritime obstacles and multiple possibilities.

As a passenger, do not expect everything to work and be patient. Ship onboard reservations might be misplaced, and glitches will appear on an inaugural voyage. Still, you get the bragging rights.

If you decide to book a maiden voyage, be aware of not having perfection, flawlessness. Yes, for the safety and sheer excitement of it all, one might not get the animal towel or drink or fancy dessert quite as anticipated.

Pack a lot of patience!

The Best Souvenir

A small sailboat with zest and adventure. A dedicated tall ship crew sharing their all.

A ship of beauty like no other. The magnificent regal schooner with hand-carved wood and fascinating history was owned by the Guinness Brewing Company. Aristotle Onassis purchased her as a wedding gift for Princess Grace and Prince Rainier. (However, he was not invited to the wedding, so the gift was not delivered.) The stunning ship did go on to become the S/V Fantome of the Windjammer Fleet.

What an experience to sail on the Fantome. We could opt to help hoist the sails and set the jibs into place by hand. We helped the crew at night to bagpipe renditions of "Amazing Grace."

Most of us slept on the open deck of teak like Angélique wood to star-watch and appreciate the roll and lure of the open seas. The morning sun brought our arrival to islands and the reality of the beauty of distant lands. We reached ports of call unreachable on big ships. Living scenes like from Treasure Island. Fresh fish on the open grill, flambé desserts, island spices, and scrumptious tasty local food. Balmy breezes complete with island music in the evenings as we sailed.

The breeze in one's face and white sails billowing bring a spiritual sense and joy. Stepping onto vacant sands with the shadows of palms swaying. For 100 cruisers = a "vacation of a lifetime."

Whether a rum swizzle, sailing memorabilia, or a hat to keep off the strength of the sun, we used doubloons for trade. The masts majestic. Wandered from waves and winds to movie-like settings of dreams and wonder.

On this schooner, when on land one day, I discovered a remarkable find. Charming Nevis is known for unsoiled palm-fringed beaches, a jewel of the West Indies. Onboard the ship had small cabins with water, yet it was impossible to keep the flow of water in the tiny shower. I have curly hair and it was an almost unattainable task to rinse my hair. There it was! Up on the rooftop! Workers high on a roof with golden bronze suntans speaking their own dialect. It was then that my eyes opened wide noticing the bungee cord and the springy triggered a thought in my mind. Made my day! I watched in awe and described a need … the handsome workers handed me one of the bungee cords.

The sound of a conch shell called us back to ship and sailing. In my hand now was my prized discovery. (Could go into business with such a thing.) I passed on the socializing and retelling of island stories and rushed straight to my cabin. Yes! The bungee cord fastened to a showerhead and a doorknob worked ideally to keep the water running. Entrepreneur? No – Simply happy with a simple discovery and a souvenir like no other.

The crew encouraged me to go out in a dingy late one afternoon. From a distance at sea, I could view the panorama and photograph the Fantome in all its beauty. It was awe-inspiring and the smiles of the crew everlasting. A picture forever in my mind to not ever forget.

Anchors aweigh! Enchanting! We never wanted the sailing to end.

The captain normally assembled us to give his salty jokes and day-to-day words – only one day they were different. Suddenly – the boat had changed course amidst sizable swells, we were whisked to land off the coast of Belize. Unexpectedly indeed. Belize is a nation of jungles and shoreline, cays, lagoons, and rich marine life. English pirates had visited these sands as well as Spanish conquistadors. On this day, however, the tapestry of the culture was not going to be explored. We sailed by one of the largest coral reef systems in the world although our arrival was not for tourism. Belizeans watched and were welcoming, though tense, as we unexpectedly disembarked and were put ashore. They implemented protective measures in hopes for our safety and actually – survival.

"A storm was brewing." Precautionary only. Captain Guyan March loved his ship, his crew, and the sea. As I look back, we had confidence in our crew, and fear did not present itself. Until – the winds began to blow and h-o-w-l. The eye of the storm was within a hundred miles of Belize. Deserted – literally on land with locals generously sharing their wisdom and help.

What I learned later was how the storm changed course constantly like a chess game for the crew and with nowhere to run. The Fantome had changed directions several times trying to escape every possible way in the open seas. Once home, colleagues, friends, and family, helped to calm my fears. "All will be fine." Until – the news showed splinters of mahogany wood and the ornate handmade wooden staircase bobbling at sea. 50-foot seas and 180-mile-per-hour-winds. Desperate. What seemed magical, became a doomed sunken ship that disappeared. Heartbreaking. That was when I knew the reality.

It was 1998, Hurricane Mitch had devastated Central America. Off the coast of Honduras, the 282-foot, 679-ton, four-masted schooner succumbed. Included were the crew of 31 who perished. A "Mayday" was reported, and it is said the Fantome went down faster than the Titanic. Heartfelt memories. Horrifying. I could never begin to imagine what that crew experienced amidst disaster and terror.

I thought to never go to sea again. Eventually, I dared to retry my fascination with the ocean. Sometimes though I can almost see those tall sails flapping in the wind and hear the sound of the soul and melody of the steel-drum music and calls of the crew. They gave me the best souvenir; they saved my life!

Last but Not Least

Mom passed away some years ago at her 93rd birthday yet is always in my thoughts. She was truly my best friend and we shared so much. When I wrote my first book (and my second and third) though I had editors, she was the one to peruse my grammar and tense. Mom attended UCLA in Los Angeles when it was a mere building on Vermont, before the UCLA as we know it today. A wise woman open to new ideas and treasured experiences. As I was writing this book and reflecting on moments and voyages, by accident I found this story my mom left for me. With tears streaming, I read her thoughts as I guess she realized that one day I would put cruising into writing. Below are the words of a 90-year-old – Miriam Small – my beloved Mom:

I Said, "YES"

It's all my fault. You see cruising is "in the blood" of my family! I was a teenager on a cruise ship with my father who was doing international business. I was all alone. I met people on the ship, and I met people on the islands where we sailed. New friends shared with me the joy of cruising.

Ports were fascinating. Every time a ship docks there is a whole new world to see. When we stopped at one island, I met a new friend and two young men. We talked about cruising and seeing so many new places. The four of us were together enjoying the colorful, unique port. Then I walked the gangway, and I went back on the ship. I saw the young men around the ship throughout our journey.

Then, just before we disembarked, one of them, James, asked me an important question. He asked me for my address. (I asked him, "Why? You never even asked me to dance!") Once reaching home and remembering the delightful details of cruising, Jim came and visited me where I lived in a small town outside of Chicago.

He came to my father and asked another very important question. Yes, the rest is – history – because when he asked me to marry him, I said, "YES." That was the beginning of a long and happy life together.

My husband was in the service and so we didn't go on many trips because of that. Nobody could. The country was at war. We had two children, Harold, and Gail. As a family, we would go together on road trips.

Eventually, we followed my parents and moved west to California. The weather in California I found to be just like a cruise. It was warmer than the east and the palm trees were beautiful.

My husband and I cruised together in later years. And, together, we danced! In those days all the passengers threw multicolored confetti while cheering, "Bon Voyage," as the ship began to glide out to sea. Cruising always reminded us of when we first met. Now since those days of past, cruise ships have gotten bigger and grander. On many ships over the years, we shared New Years and splendid special occasions.

I had the pleasure of taking each of my four grandchildren on a ship, one at a time. It was such a special way to share and build a grandparent/grandchild relationship. Each cruise was a treasure all its own. When traveling with my youngest grandchild, Michael, we stood at the railing and joined passengers and crew in loud cheers of celebration when the ship saved someone stranded at sea.

When James passed away, I cherished the memories we had shared on the ocean. I continued to cruise with my son and his family as well as with my daughter too. Gail now speaks on cruises thus sharing her writing talent while inspiring others. She continues to love cruising and her husband Dave, and son, Michael, enjoy the adventure of the seas and relaxation. They just want to know, "When is the next cruise?" I, myself, stopped counting cruises knowing that each one is an extraordinary adventure at sea.

My late brother, Benjamin, went on a getaway voyage when young. He met his lovely wife at sea. There must be something in the water as we both had the fortune of beautiful marriages and cherished voyages.

I sailed with Gail on the original Love Boat. We were even looking for Doc and Isaac with excitement because of the popular television show we always watched together. There also was the cruise when the Macarena was first introduced in Europe. The cruise staff taught it to the passengers and every room one went into, even at High Tea, the Macarena music played. Gail brought the dance and tune back to America and taught a version of it to the 600 children at the school where she taught.

I have sailed already to most continents and to places far and near around the world. I used to collect pictures of me meeting each ship's captain on those gala captain's nights. I always liked the captain's party because you can hear the words of the master of the vessel, each with a different accent to share. It is also a chance to toast with new friends and strangers to a wonderful cruise filled with health and smooth sailing.

A silly hobby I developed while traveling to ports, countries, and varied destinations is to take a picture next to a policeman.

They usually oblige and it is quite interesting when later looking through photo albums to observe the different uniforms, styles, and stance.

Room service is a welcome treat to feel spoiled and lazy. Why not? On the day I sailed through the Panama Canal it was a splendid view through the porthole of the glistening sea and historical sight.

I think the cruise staff, waiters, and room stewards make each voyage what it is. It is fun to talk to them and hear their array of stories. They have the talent of finding ways to make everything special. Whether it be an extra Caesar salad for Gail, Hal interacting with the wine sommelier, games for those daring and silly, or a towel folded into an animal upon returning to the cabin late at night, the enjoyable experience is there for all to have.

Gail took me cruising this past year to celebrate my turning ninety years old. At age ninety, I think that Antarctica sounds a little too cold for me. Maybe it is time now to settle down and just tell my multitude of stories.

Cruising involves attitude. Laughing enhances each journey and is the secret to cruising and calmness on the seas. Cruising to Europe with Gail the airlines lost our luggage. It was Good Friday, Easter Sunday, and Easter Monday all in the first three days of our arrival. We had no choice but to have hope –

and to laugh. Gail found a swank hotel and bought me a warm outfit since a cold storm had blown in. Her wrap-around skirt – unwrapped – and that was all she had to wear. A fellow passenger, a total stranger, knocked on our cabin door. When I opened it, she looked at us and handed Gail an elegant outfit to wear for the evening saying, "I think this is exactly your size." That is an example of what cruising is all about, the unexpected moments that create lasting memories.

My advice: Everyone should go on a cruise because cruising is interesting and fun. No two cruises are ever the same. On each voyage, you meet new people and see interesting places. It is a great way to see the world! You can be anywhere you want to be on an ocean voyage. You can be who you want to be at some of the costume parties aboard. Once my husband dressed up as a pregnant woman and kept looking at his watch. He won a prize while having fun at the same time. As each cruise comes to an end, it is then that you should begin to dream of the next cruise.

When asked what I like best on a ship, my answer has to be that I like the chocolate the best. It comes in every shape and size. Cruise ships have a wonderful buffet for tasting those scrumptious chocolate treats. Shiny foil chocolate mints appearing nightly on the pillow are a welcome surprise. I've also had chocolate fondue, cookies, chocolate-covered strawberries, and steaming hot chocolate while sailing amidst glaciers. That is my secret for staying young!

I remember the twinkling lights in the night on a cruise ship that almost dance as they sparkle and reflect on the ocean. Now I get postcards from Gail from every port she visits. I travel with her in thought and can't wait for her stories and pictures upon her return.

A Special Thank You

To all the people I have met on voyages
that make cruising what it is!

To Cindy Mihaly for your assistance
as an extraordinary editor ...

To David Endelman, my husband, who
is there for me sharing so much, and his
creativity that enhances mine

To those sharing adventures of voyages with
me: Annie, Bette, Carrie, Cathie, Clare, Dave,
Ellen, Lynne, Michael, Mom, Nellie, and Toni

About the Author
Gail Small

With extensive travel through the seven seas to all five continents, Gail Small champions the joy of journeys and the adventure of living! Her books and presentations provide insight into the power of choice to navigate life. She is an author, speaker, educator, and consultant. She has true and amazing stories to tell.

Gail is the author of *Joyful Learning, Joyful Parenting,* and *Joyful Volunteering.* She has also written three books for children and is a contributor to *Chicken*

Soup for the Soul. She is an innovative educator, Fulbright Memorial Scholar, and Bravo award recipient. Ms. Small holds a Master's in Education and Certification with the William Glasser Institute.

Gail has been on 101 plus cruises. She is featured on cruise ships around the world and at national and international conferences on topics such as the art of travel, communication, creativity, writing, and choice theory.

Gail loves animals, the color yellow, fresh salads, Zumba, and watching sunsets at sea.

For more, go to:
gailsmall.com

Made in the USA
Las Vegas, NV
01 September 2021

29401203R00132